BILLY SUNDAY

The Life and Work of the Baseball Evangelist—

The Real Billy Sunday

ELIJAH P. BROWN, D. D.

AMBASSADOR INTERNATIONAL

GREENVILLE, SOUTH CAROLINA & BELFAST, NORTHERN IRELAND

Billy Sunday
The Life and Work of the Baseball Evangelist—The Real Billy Sunday

ISBN 1 932307 55 9

Published by the Ambassador Group

Ambassador International
427 Wade Hampton Blvd.
Greenville, SC 29609
USA
www.emeraldhouse.com

and

Ambassador Publications Ltd.
Providence House
Ardenlee Street
Belfast BT6 8QJ
Northern Ireland
www.ambassador-productions.com

The colophon is a trademark of Ambassador

This book has been written by a
friend who has known me nearly
all my Christian life.
He has brought to the task a ripe
experience as a Christian, an
Evangelist, and a Literary man.
The reader will find he has
performed his duty well.

W. A. Sunday.
2. Tim. 2:15.

CONTENTS

ILLUSTRATIONS

INTRODUCTORY

THE making of this book has not been undertaken as a defense of Mr. Sunday, for he needs none; the Master whom he so energetically serves having put His seal upon his labors in a way that the whole continent has been compelled to take note of. But the book is put into the hand of the reader with the hope and the prayer that through it he may come to know the real Billy Sunday, and learn how wondrously the Lord of Hosts is using him.

I undertook this work believing that I ought to do it. Some years ago I was with Mr. Sunday as his confidential assistant, and so came to know him intimately. This made me conversant with the way in which his great campaigns are conducted, and gave me a knowledge of the details and machinery of his meetings. Having been a student of character all my life, I do not believe any other man has a clearer comprehension of the real Sunday than myself. Others who have been associated with him may possibly know him as well, but I am confident no one can know him better.

I made his acquaintance soon after his conversion, and have kept in touch with him ever since. I have summered and wintered with him. Have eaten and slept with him. I have seen him in the limelight and in private life. I know his great passion for souls, and how it drives him to pour out his life and strength in trying to win them. I know how he preaches and what he preaches for. I know how he lives, and I know how

11

he gives, and I know that he hasn't a drop of mercenary blood in his veins. I know how he tithes every dollar of his income. I know how religiously and quietly he is continually doing good with his money. I know of many struggling ones whose hearts he gladdens with timely help; of missions and struggling causes he aids, and I know of poor families supported by his bounty.

I know that however unconventional his language may be, his preaching has in it the spirit of Christ and the power of Christ, and that it accomplishes what Christ commissioned His disciples to do. I know that he believes the Bible to be the word of God, and believes himself to be a messenger from God. I know that he fears neither man nor devil when he stands in the pulpit, and if it came to a test would go to the stake for his faith. A more honest or zealous man I have never known. He puts his very life and soul into every message he gives, and has kept on the go nearly all the year round for years without rest.

This is the man in whose wake new buildings spring up for churches and Christian Associations for both young men and young women. The man who quickens the religious life of every church within fifty miles of where he preaches; even of those that antagonize his meetings. This is the man whose preaching makes religion something more than a name to conjure with. This is the man whom not only the common people, but all kinds of people hear gladly, because they can understand him.

This is the man whose preaching makes people pay debts that have been outlawed, and brings long separated husbands and wives together in loving reconciliation. The preaching that fills every church in the community with new life and new blood; makes a market for Bibles by the ten thousand, and makes religion the chief topic of conversation everywhere. His preaching creates respect for the Sabbath and the house of God; makes it easier to enforce the laws; reduces crime, and slaps the devil squarely in the face wherever he shows his cloven hoof. It closes saloons and opens prayer meetings, and rekindles the fire on burnt out family altars.

Mr. Sunday is not an uncertainty or an experiment. From his first meeting to his last he has had unbroken success. He has never held a meeting that did not result in a revival that reached the whole community, and he has never preached in a building large enough to admit all who thronged to hear him. There were places where Moody failed, and there have been places where all great evangelists have failed, but Sunday has never failed anywhere. He has been holding great evangelistic meetings for almost twenty years, nearly every one in a tabernacle built especially for it, and almost every meeting has been greater than the last. His converts are numbered by multitudes, and will compare with those who have accepted Christ in any meeting.

Nicodemus was not blind in both eyes when he said to Jesus: " No man can do these miracles that thou doest except God be with him." And this is the message the Master gave to the disciples of John the Baptist: " Go your way, and tell John what things ye have seen and heard; how the blind see, the lame walk, the lepers are cleansed, the dead are raised, to the poor the gospel is preached." Try Billy Sunday by this test, and every unprejudiced Christian man will be compelled to admit that he is a man sent of God.

ELIJAH P. BROWN.

SUNDAY'S FIRST HOME.

I

SUNDAY'S BIRTH AND BOYHOOD

IN a little log cabin of two rooms, floored with rough boards, a fireplace of flagstones, a chimney of unbarked logs plastered with clay, small windows and a low-hung roof—the typical home of the midwestern pioneer—in these lowly surroundings was born William Ashley Sunday, to whom it has been given as to no other American to turn many to righteousness.

This humble dwelling is still standing in Story County, Iowa, a mile and a half south of the city of Ames. Four months before his birth, on November 19, 1862, his father, William Sunday, marched away from his home, to the sound of fife and drum, a soldier of the Union. The father never came back. Death ended his service, and his grave is unknown.

Edward Sunday, a brother now living in North Dakota, was two years old when William was born. Albert, two years older than Edward, died in 1893.

Previous to the birth of his son William Sunday wrote home from the front that if his child were a boy, he wanted him to be called William Ashley. This was done, though no member of the family has been able to tell why the middle name of Ashley was chosen.

William Sunday was a contractor and brickmason. He built one of the first brick buildings in Cedar Rapids, Iowa; a house that is still standing. He was also a violinist of considerable repute. When the call came for volunteers he enlisted at once. In fording a stream he was wet to the skin, contracted a severe cold, from the effects of which he died in camp, probably of pneumonia. He was buried at Camp Patterson, Mo. His body was afterward, it is believed, removed to a new resting-place near Washington Barracks, at St. Louis. Persistent efforts have been made in recent years to identify this grave, but without success. William Sunday had a sister, Mary Simmons, who went as a pioneer with him.

The babyhood days of William Ashley were spent in the log cabin. The burden of the family rested heavily upon the soldier's widow. Yet with a true mother's heroism she faced the trying situation bravely, and struggled as only a mother can to keep her babies together. For a time she succeeded, but no one will ever know all the heartaches, cares and distresses endured by her in those trying days. Yet that she lived true to the duties of motherhood, rearing her boys in the way they should go, and inculcating principles of truth and righteousness, is happily evident to-day. This mother is now a loved and revered member of the evangelist's family circle.

During the first three years of his life Billy was anything but a healthy child, and his mother and her relatives often despaired of his life. He was small at birth, lacking in strength, and for some reason did not gain rapidly, as his brothers had done. Then an old French doctor, living in the neighborhood, prescribed some herb remedies that seemed to be just the thing, for they soon had the boy going toward robust health. This is probably the reason why he often gives expression to a theory that in weeds, herbs and shrubs will some day be found the cure for all the ills that flesh is heir to.

A farmer in the neighborhood gave the little boy one of the first jobs he ever had. He rode one of the lead horses of a four-horse team hitched to a reaper for eight days, for twenty-five cents a day. When the child reached home at the end of the work he was sore in every part of his little body, and his eyes had been almost blinded by the sun, but he was happy in the possession of a two-dollar bill. His cup of joy was made to run clear over when he found that while he had been away his mother had made for him his first hickory shirt.

Sunday had a half-sister whose death came, some time before this, from burns received in a bonfire accident. His mother had a small picture of this sister, and in his boyish impulsiveness, he at once decided to spend his hardly earned two dollars in having it enlarged and framed. This crayon enlargement is still in possession of the family.

A feature of Sunday's boyhood, which he remembers well, had to do with a sugarcane mill built and operated by his grandfather. This mill was a rude device used to crush and squeeze the sap from the cane. A raw-boned swaybacked plug of a horse, going round and round in a ring, furnished the motive power, and Albert, Edward and Will took turns as engineers. Then the boys, when mere youngsters, learned to tend the fires, which boiled the sap to the consistency of thick sorghum molasses. After the juice once began to boil it had to be kept going without cooling until finished. Otherwise it was about sure to sour.

While the boiling was going on a great deal of skimming had to be done, to take out the impurities thus brought to the surface. This often kept the fires going late into the night, and sometimes till after midnight. These sugaring-off nights in the heart of a western wood were just what a boy liked, and that is why they are so well remembered. The boys learned to cut wood, build fences, care for horses on the farm of their grandfather, and milk ten or a dozen cows a day.

When Sunday was a small boy, he was one day hailed on the street by a man who had the reputation of being as tight as the bark on a tree.

"Do you know burdock, sonny?" asked the man.

"Sure I do," said Billy.

"My wife is sick. Get me a good bunch of it quick, and I'll give you a nickel."

Away went the boy on the run to his home on the farm two miles away, and was soon busy in a big patch of burdock. In a remarkably short time he had a hatful of fine roots, which he carefully washed, and then hurried with them to his man, but only to hear him say:

"I don't need 'em now, bub. Another fellow come along with plenty of burdock, and I got all I wanted from him."

The poor boy instantly felt the milk of human kindness sour in him, and going slowly to the creek, he threw the roots into the deepest place he could find, and then stoned them until the last bitter root sank out of sight. He remembers no greater disappointment of his boyhood days.

Thirty years later Sunday was preaching to a great audience in a town in Iowa, and "old Burdock" was in the meeting. He told every one near him that he knew the preacher when he was a little boy, and at the close he went up and made as much fuss over Billy as he would have done had he been his own son. Sunday of course remembered the man and his meanness, in swindling a child out of his hard-earned nickel.

Billy was one day out in the garden with his grandfather, and for a time both were busy pulling weeds—and then the most casual observer would have seen with one eye that only the grandsire was diligent. It was one of the hardest days anybody ever saw for a little boy to be thrifty. It was such a fine balmy day that fish would almost jump out of the water to bite, and soon Billy's thoughts and desires were more than a mile and a half away from that truck patch.

His grandfather was weeding away so busily that he failed to notice that the boy wasn't keeping up with his row, and was rather startled when he looked up and saw the little dreamer sitting in the shade under a currant bush.

" Hello, son; what are you doing there? " queried the old gentleman.

" I was just a-thinking, grandfather."

" Thinking? Thinking about what? "

" Thinking about what I'm going to do when I get to be a man."

" And what do you think you are going to do then? "

" I think I'm not going to pull weeds when I get to be a man. I'm going to hunt around and find a good job I can work at with my head."

And he certainly kept his word, though he probably exercises about every muscle in his body every time he preaches. At all events his exertion keeps him in such splendid physical trim that he can go out and play a game of baseball without being sore.

One newspaper had a careful estimate made, and declared that Sunday traveled a mile in every sermon, and covered something over a hundred miles on the platform in every campaign.

Many of the incidents of Sunday's boyhood which would delight readers to-day have slipped from his mother's memory, but one in particular she remembers clearly.

When he was only three or four years old his grandmother died, and her death and burial in midwinter made a deep impression upon the child. The graveyard was only a few hundred yards from the home, and one morning, several days after the funeral, the mother missed the boy, but found it easy to trace him by his little footprints in the snow. She found him at the grave of his grandmother, kneeling beside it and saying a little prayer she had taught him.

Billy went to the neighborhood school, the typical country district school, where the pupils sat on rough benches and learned the " Three R's " after a much ruder fashion than is known to-day. Later he went to one of the grade schools in Ames.

Finding it impossible to longer give the boys the proper care at home, and believing that it would give them a much better chance in life, the mother of Edward and William decided, though with much reluctance, to send them to the Soldiers' Orphans Home, at Glenwood, Iowa. In one of his sermons Sunday most touchingly tells the tender story of the parting:

" Four months before I was born my father went to the war, in Company E of the Twenty-third Iowa. I have fought and struggled since I was six years old. I know all about the dark and seamy side of life. If a man ever fought for everything he gained, I have. The wolf scratched at the cabin door, and scratched so hard that finally my poor mother had to say to my brother Ed and me—

" ' Boys, I'm going to send you to the Soldiers' Orphans Home!'

" She took us to Ames, where we had to wait a long

WILLIAM SUNDAY. FATHER OF THE EVANGELIST.

time for the train. We went to a little hotel near the depot to wait. About one o'clock in the morning somebody came and said—

"'Get ready for the train; it's coming.'

"I looked into my mother's face. Her eyes were red with long weeping, for the poor woman didn't have money enough to pay our fare all the way to Glenwood, where the Home was.

"We went to the train, where mother put one arm around me, and the other about Ed, and sobbed as if her poor heart would break. People walked by, looked at us, but they didn't say a word. Why? They didn't know, and if they had they wouldn't have cared. But mother knew; yes, and she knew that for four years she wouldn't see her boys.

"We got into a car, and said, 'Good-by, mother,' as the train started, and it was the first good-by to her I had ever said. The last we saw of her she was smiling upon us through her tears. Yes; mother knew, and mother cared.

"We reached Council Bluffs early in the morning. It was cold, and we turned our little thin coat collars up around our necks and shivered. We saw a little hotel, and going to it we asked a woman we saw there for something to eat. She asked our names, and I said:

"'My name is Willie Sunday, and this is my brother Ed.'

"'And where are you going?' she then asked.

"'To the Soldiers' Orphans Home at Glenwood,' I told her.

"She wiped her eyes, and said, 'My husband was a soldier, and he never came back. He wouldn't turn any one away, and I surely won't turn you boys away.'

"She put her arms about us, and said, 'Come on in.'

"She gave us our breakfast, and our dinner too. There was no train out on the Burlington till afternoon. We played around in the freight yards until near the time, when we saw a freight train standing on the track, and climbed into the caboose. After the train started the conductor came along, and said:

"'Where are your tickets?'

"'Ain't got any,' said I.

"'Where's your money?'

"'Ain't got any.'

"'Then I'll have to put you off,' he said.

"We commenced to cry. My brother Ed handed him a letter of introduction to the superintendent of the Home. As he read it his eyes filled with tears, and as he handed it back, he said:

"'Just sit still, boys; it won't cost you a cent to ride on my train.'

"It is twenty miles from Council Bluffs to Glenwood, and as we rounded the curve the conductor said:

"'There is the Home on the hill, boys!' The conductor often visited us at the Home, and never failed to give us candy, peanuts and pennies. He was afterwards killed not far from the Home.

"We were there about a year and a half when the Home was discontinued, and the children, about sixty in all—were transferred to the Orphans' Home at Davenport, Iowa."

In the Davenport Home young Billy had the advantage of good schooling and proper religious instruction, and in the systematic atmosphere he found there, he was inspired with an ambition to make something out of himself. There he was taught to be earnest and energetic, painstaking and thorough in whatever he undertook.

A strong religious influence filled the place, and what

he was taught there of religion and the Bible was sufficent to make him a believer in the divine authority of the Scriptures. So well and skillfully was he filled with Bible knowledge that he has ever since been free from all intellectual doubt, although he did not become a Christian until after he reached man's estate. He will never cease to be thankful for the years he spent in the Davenport Home, and the molding influence it exerted upon all his after life.

Sunday's mother was a Christian woman, and although she did not long have him under her care, like the mother of Samuel she turned his little feet into the right pathway.

One incident connected with Billy's stay at the Glenwood Home reveals the bent of the boy's mind at the time, and shows why he has waged lifelong antagonism against oppression of the weak by the strong. In the school were boys of various dispositions, one of whom was the typical beefy bully; a boy who lorded it over the others just because he thought he could. Billy had never had any trouble with this boy himself, but it stirred him to the quick to see how arrogantly and overbearing he behaved toward the others.

Finally it was decided in a little group of boys that this state of affairs must stop, and it fell on Billy to champion the cause of the weak.

He felt sure that he could lick the bully, and was more than willing to try. Fighting in school was of course against the rules, but some nights later the bully was " dared to come out." So about three o'clock in the morning, out crept a dozen or more of the youngsters, clad only in their night shirts and trousers, and stealthily made their way, through windows and down waterpipes, to the protecting shadow of a clump of trees well removed from the school building.

In the dim light before the dawn they formed a ring, and the bully went into it with a chip on his shoulder. But zip! that moment Billy sent it flying, and before the bully could get over his astonishment, rapid and telling blows from Billy's fist were being planted in his beefy face.

With the agility of a cat the smaller boy danced this way and that, on the alert for openings, into which he shot with all the energy his body held. The fast and furious conflict, in all of which Billy was giving the bully a lot of punishment, tickled the other boys mightily, until the snob was given all he deserved. The victory was to Billy, and the bully was quite a different boy afterward. That early morning drubbing was probably the making of him.

At the Glenwood school a strict rule required prompt appearance at meals, and boys who were not on hand to the dot had to miss both that meal and the next. Somehow or other Billy found it hard to obey that rule. In later years he has generally been " Johnny on the spot," but in that time he had to miss a good many meals.

To miss two meals a day is not a good thing for a growing boy, and it began to show on Billy so much that it greatly worried his brother Ed. The older boy was as anxious to have his little brother look well as the king's steward was that Daniel should, and so Ed began to scratch his head and do some thinking himself.

In his scratching he must have touched the right spot, for he soon managed to have himself assigned to the task of cleaning the kitchen. When his work there was finished it fell upon him to lock the door. This he faithfully did, but it often happened that little Billy was locked in the kitchen. The plate he had missed at the table Ed would tuck away in some convenient corner, and in spite of his tardiness Billy waxed fat and strong, and soon began to have a countenance as ruddy as that of David when he stood before Samuel.

Revival meetings always had a fascination for Sunday, and he cannot remember a time when he did not like to attend them, though in his young life he never had a thought of himself becoming an evangelist.

On his mother's side Sunday is descended from Lord William Corey, who married the only daughter of Sir Francis Drake. Both of his great-grandfathers on the maternal side fought in the Revolutionary War. One lost a leg under Anthony Wayne at Brandywine, and the other fought under Hull at Detroit. His grandfather and General Grant were boys together. His grandparents on his father's side were born in Germany. They settled in Pennsylvania, and his father was born in that state, not far from Chambersburg.

II

SUNDAY LEAVES THE DAVENPORT HOME

SUNDAY left the Home at Davenport when he was fourteen years old. Boys were discharged by age limitation at sixteen, and his brother Ed, being two years older, had remained his full time. The two brothers were so much to each other that Billy couldn't think of being left alone, and so chose to depart with Ed.

The boys went to live with their grandfather on a farm near Ames. Squire Corey was one of the pioneer settlers in the state. He was a man of hard common-sense, and of a rough and ready stamp. He was somewhat brusque and blunt in his ways, and seldom had much to say, a trait in which his famous grandson is much like him.

As a boy Sunday had the same highstrung nervous nature that characterizes him to-day, and there were times when the seeming harshness of his grandfather cut him to the quick. But in his heart the old gentleman had a lot of real goodness, and had a great love for Billy. He showed much concern for the boy's best interests, and gave him good counsel, which, being remembered, exerted a wholesome influence on all his after life.

Sunday's mother remembers how he was always his grandfather's favorite, and she tells how proudly he would set him on his shoulder, when he was not much more than big enough to run alone, and go marching down the road with the boy holding on to him by the hair, just as he would take a horse by the mane whenever he was set on its back. Sunday still remembers the days he spent on his grandfather's farm as, in the main, the happiest in his boyhood life.

His grandfather was a most genial and big-hearted man. He never turned any one from the door hungry. He was of the pioneer type, and was one of the earliest settlers in the state of Iowa, having located there in 1848. He was the only father Sunday ever knew, and he speaks of him with tender affection to this day. He never goes near the city of Ames but that he visits the old home, and goes out to the old cemetery on the farm.

Here is one instance of the way in which his grandfather's counsel has remained with him: The neighborhood was stirred by interest in a spelling match, in which the young people from several counties were to take part. Some days before the time a friend of the Sunday boys boasted that he was going to wear a white store collar to the spelling match. To Billy the white store collar seemed to be about the finest thing that could be thought of, and so he went to his grandfather about it.

" Listen to me, son," said the old man; " it is not what you wear on you, but what you have in you that makes a man. Be honest, and do your work with all your might, and then some day you won't have to wear a white collar to make folks look up to you."

The boy caught the idea, and was so cheered by it that he went to the spelling bee in a happy and contented frame of mind. Often in talking to the young he quotes the words of his grandfather, to help and encourage them: " It is not what you have on you, but what you have in you that makes a man."

But in many ways life on a farm did not appeal very strongly to Billy. He was ill at ease there, and often felt that his career would have to be found in some other calling. This decision was brought to a climax one day by a trivial thing that happend most unexpectedly.

The grandfather sent Billy and his half-brother to the barn to carry a neck yoke to the field. As they were doing this, the big ring at one end of the yoke suddenly came loose, and without any fault of theirs. The boys got the blame, however, and a severe tongue lashing to boot.

This fired the highstrung Billy, and right there and then he decided to leave the farm, and for good. His brother, with tears in his eyes, begged him not to go, but his dander was up and he stood firm.

If the angels know anything about the future, there must have been some joy in heaven over the breaking of that neck yoke, for had it held together only a little longer the man who sways multitudes now might not have been a preacher.

With what little money he had in his jeans, Billy next morning hired a horse from a neighbor, and rode seven miles to Nevada on the hunt for a job. He found a place as utility boy in a little fourth-rate hotel.

He had to meet all the trains, and often carry grips that strong men were glad to put down. He swept and did every other little odd job about the place that no one else was willing to do. In the daytime he was on duty in the dingy, stuffy office, reeking with tobacco smoke and bad stories, and at night he slept behind the counter. He stuck to this job eight months, and received as pay his board and lodging. He was then allowed to take a day off to go and visit his grandfather. He stayed on the farm two days instead of one, and for doing so lost the place. On his return the landlord even denied him entrance to the office, but his wife be-

MOTHER OF THE EVANGELIST.

friended the boy. She let him in through the back door, and gave him a meal and his lodging for the night.

The next day Sunday learned that Col. John Scott, once lieutenant-governor of Iowa, wanted to hire a boy. He went to the Scott home and asked for the job. Col. Scott called his wife in, and together they looked the boy over. Billy caught the Colonel's fancy at once, but Mrs. Scott was not so sure, so she said:

" You may go and scrub the cellar stairs for me, son."

Billy went at the job with a smile that covered his whole face, for if there was anything he was strong at, it was the scrubbing of cellar stairs. Had he been asked to pick out his own job for a try-out, it would have been the very thing he was told to do. He had learned that trade, and learned it well, at the Orphans' Home, for he had to do a lot of it there.

He has never done anything in his life, from licking a bully to skinning the devil, but what he did it thoroughly and to a finish, and in that same way he cleaned those cellar stairs. The moment Mrs. Scott looked at them she gave the casting vote for Billy.

Among his other duties in the Scott home, he took care of twenty Shetland ponies. In this place he got eight dollars a month and his board and lodging.

During a meeting he held at Steubenville, Ohio, in 1913, Sunday heard that Mrs. Rex, a sister of Col. Scott, lived there. He and Mrs. Sunday went to visit her, and had a very pleasant day. Sunday preached in Richmond, Ohio, where Col. Scott was born, and the little church was packed to the doors, and twenty-four were converted. Edwin M. Stanton, Secretary of War under Lincoln, was born at Steubenville, and so also were the McCooks, who were renowned generals during the Civil War. In his early life Col. Scott had lived in that part of

Ohio and from the large part he had had in Sunday's early career, the people of Richmond felt that the evangelist was one of their very own, and did their best to make him feel at home.

There was a good school in the Home at Davenport, and while there Sunday had passed the grades, and so was able to enter the high school at Nevada, which he did while working for Col. Scott. He completed the course, maintaining all the way through a high average of scholarship. His memory's marvelous retentive powers were displayed early.

During the last two years of his high school course he had the job of janitor of the school building. This compelled him to leave his bed at three o'clock in the morning during the winter, start fourteen fires and keep them going during the day. For those fires he also had to carry the coal, do the sweeping and dusting, and whatever else was needed in the care of the building.

From his early boyhood Sunday was a great runner, and always racing with other boys. At a Fourth of July celebration at Ames, when he was thirteen, he won the first prize in a footrace that was open to all. The prize he won was three dollars, and no three dollars ever looked any bigger to a boy. His strongest competitor in the race that day was a young man from the Agricultural College. The student ran in racing togs, and Billy with bare feet.

During his high school days at Nevada, his speed as a runner began to attract much attention, and no wonder, for later he was to be one of the first men in the country to do a hundred yards in ten seconds.

When his high school course was finished he was persuaded to go to Marshalltown, so that he might be a member of the Marshalltown Fire Brigade. Firemen's tournaments were then very popular all over the state, and largely attended wherever held. Sunday had had a part in some of these, and was beginning to be known as a young man of remarkable speed, and as fleetness of foot was the thing that was at a premium in the winning teams, the Marshalltown Fire Brigade was determined to have him.

His first job in Marshalltown was in an undertaking and furniture shop. He liked it no better than he had done farming, and especially detested varnishing chairs, and it was what he had to do the most. One day his employer, who stood watching him, said:

" That's not the way to do it; let me show you." Then after a few strokes of the brush, he said:

" Can't you do it that way? "

" Not on your life," said Billy, " or I wouldn't be working for you for three dollars a week."

While in Marshalltown, Sunday became interested in baseball, and played with the city team. This marks one of the significant points in his career. He played a spectacular game from the start, and his base running was astonishing. It was in the early eighties that Anson discovered Sunday at Marshalltown, and it came about in this way: Some time before Billy's playing in Marshalltown the Club had won for it the State Championship of Local Clubs. The game was with Des Moines, and was played in the Fair Grounds at Des Moines.

They told Anson so much about this game, and Sunday's fine playing in it, that the Captain sat up and took notice that Billy must be something out of the ordinary as a player, and right there the young man's long lane of hard luck took a short turn for the better.

Anson had been born and reared in Marshalltown,

and at that time was spending some time there, visiting his father. He had an aunt, known to many familiarly as " Aunt Em," and it was she who drew the Captain's attention to Sunday. And but for the interest this good woman took in him, Billy might have remained in that furniture shop varnishing chairs for years, with a loathing like that Israel came to have for quail. Or if Anson had not made that most timely visit to the home of his boyhood, the man who is now preaching to such vast multitudes might have evoluted into a solemn-faced undertaker, who could be happy only when putting crape on the door.

Anson had a meeting with Sunday, and was not long in convincing him that his forte lay, not in driving a hearse or selling crape at two dollars a yard, but in giving his legs a chance to do their best on the diamond, and so once more Billy packed his grip and boarded the cars to go to Chicago, where he landed with only a dollar in his pocket, but with hope beating high in his breast. Arrived there, he was soon wearing the uniform of the famous old White Stockings, of the National League, the club that won the championship for the windy city every year but two in the period of 1883-7.

On the Chicago team at that time were Flint and Kelly, catchers; Clarkson and McCormick, pitchers; Anson, Pfeffer, Burns and Williamson, the " stonewall " infield, with Dalrymple, Gore and Sunday in the outfield.

This was brisk company, but Billy was soon admittedly the fastest runner, not only in the Chicago team, but in the profession. He was the first man who ever ran the bases in fourteen seconds. Anson has always contended that he was the fastest baserunner who ever played the game. It is remarkable that he went straight from the

STATE OF IOWA

ADJUTANT-GENERAL'S OFFICE

It Is Certified, That the Records of this office show that _William Sunday_, Age _34_, Nativity _Penna._, residence _Edge Farm, Story Co._, Iowa, was enlisted in Company _"E"_, (Captain _John C. Lininger_) _23rd_ Regiment Iowa Vol. _Inf._ on the _14th_ day of _August_, 186_2_, and was mustered into the United States service as a _private_ for the period of _3_ years, on _22nd_ day of _August_, 186_2_; at _Des Moines, Iowa_, by _Lt. Chas J. Ball_, U. S. A. Mustering Officer, and that the said _William Sunday_ _died of disease December 22d 1862_ _at Camp Patterson, Missouri._

IN TESTIMONY WHEREOF, witness my hand and seal, at Des Moines, this _10_ day of _May_, 190_9_.

Guy E. Logan
Adjutant-General.

NO FEES ARE CHARGED FOR THESE CERTIFICATES

CERTIFIED COPY OF RECORD IN ADJUTANT-GENERAL'S OF-
FICE, STATE OF IOWA, SHOWING ENLISTMENT AND
DEATH OF MR. SUNDAY'S FATHER.

prairie into the Major League, without any probation in a Minor League.

The same forcefulness and remarkable energy which now mark Sunday's evangelistic efforts were just as prominent in his career on the diamond. He was always conscientious, painstaking and suggestive, and a brilliant outfielder, but it was his wonderful speed in running bases for which he was most remarkable.

Anson's confidence in Sunday was shown by the fact that he turned over to him the responsibility connected with much of the business management of the Chicago Club, this more particularly when on the road. Sunday collected the percentages, figured out the railroad routes, and made hotel arrangements. He often carried thousands of dollars around with him in a satchel.

Speaking of Sunday, in his baseball book, Anson says:

" The first thirteen times that Sunday went to the bat after he began playing with the Chicagos, he struck out, but I was convinced that he would yet make a ball player, and hung on to him, cheering him up as best I could whenever he became discouraged. As a base runner his judgment was at times faulty, and he was altogether too daring, taking extraordinary chances because of the tremendous turn of speed he possessed. He was a good fielder, and a strong and accurate thrower, his weak point lying in his batting.

" The ball that he threw was a hard one to catch, however, it landing in the hands like a chunk of lead. As a thrower, he was not swift as Clarkson, Pfeffer or Burns, all of whom sent the ball across the field with the speed of a bullet, and with the accuracy of first-class marksmen. In spite of the extreme speed with which they came into the hands, however, they seemed to sort o' lift themselves as they came, and so landed lightly, while the ball thrown by Sunday, to the contrary, seemed to gain in weight as it sailed through the air, and was heavy and soggy when it struck the hands. This is strange, but a fact, and one which perhaps some scientist can explain.

"Sunday was, in my opinion, the strongest man in the profession on his feet, and could run the bases like a frightened deer. His greatest lack as a ball player was his inability to bat as well as some of the hard-hitting outfielders. He was a fast and brilliant fielder, a fine thrower, and once on first he could steal more bases than any of his team mates."

III

THE BASEBALL PLAYER'S CONVERSION

THE remarkable vitality and buoyant energy which mark Sunday's preaching are the same as characterized his work on the diamond and other activities years ago. His elasticity and recuperative power have always amazed and puzzled his friends. He seems to have a quality of endurance that makes him well-nigh superhuman. A rallying force that never fails him, and makes him equal to the terrific strain of one hard campaign after another, with scarcely any rest between them. This must be due in great measure to the blood of iron and constitution of steel he inherited from his mother.

The early days of her young motherhood were spent in the turmoil and struggle of pioneer life. She was not enfeebled by the poison of bad air, so common to modern life, for no better ventilated dwelling was ever known than the log cabin of the early settler. Then, too, she had the advantage of being able to spend much time in God's great out-of-doors, drinking in health and strength from the life-giving sunshine.

This, with plain and wholesome food and pure water, equipped her well to transmit a good physical heritage to her children. When God wants to raise up a man with power to shake the world, he sees to it that he shall have the right kind of a mother, and this was especially true of Billy Sunday.

The daily routine of Sunday's life has always been

such as would develop his muscle, but not exhaust it. Another great thing in his favor is that he has not been handicapped with bad habits. His manhood has never been sapped by dissipation. He has never been lax in his morals or life, but has always held the rein of self-control upon himself. He never used tobacco in any form. Had he been a cigarette fiend he would have been down and out long ago. He never had any appetite for liquor. During his early baseball days, when out with his team mates, he may have taken a glass of wine or beer sometimes, but it was his habit to use only soft drinks.

In his eating he is also just as temperate. He favors the most simply prepared foods, and seldom drinks anything but weak tea and coffee. He is a light eater, but generally when in a meeting eats four meals a day, the last being a small lunch about an hour after the close of the evening service. He also gets along with surprisingly little sleep, and claims that he can hold his own with Edison on that line.

This is one of the things that endeared Sunday to the baseball public: He bubbled over and sparkled with sheer vitality. Anson often said he might as well try to hold a frightened deer as undertake to restrain Sunday when he made up his mind to leave one base and fly to the next.

His fleetness of foot attracted attention elsewhere than on the diamond. For Anson was in the habit of backing him against all comers. In one of his sermons Sunday tells the following story:

" Before I was converted Anson had backed me for a hundred-yard race with ' Arlie ' Latham of the St. Louis ' Browns,' for five hundred dollars a side and the gate money, to be run at St. Louis one Sunday at the end of the season, and this bothered me a lot, I tell you.

"I prayed over it night after night, but I couldn't see my way clear. I didn't want to do it, but how was I to get out of it? Finally I went to 'Pop' Anson and told him he would have to let me out.

"'Why, Billy,' he said, 'you're not going to be yellow, and a quitter, are you?'

"I explained to him, but he wouldn't listen.

"'No, Billy,' he said, 'I've backed you for a thousand dollars in this race, and so have a lot of my friends. There's about seventy-five thousand dollars up on it. I'm not much on religion, but I don't believe that God wants you to start out with him by throwing down your friends, on a contract that you took before you went with him. Now I tell you what you do. You go down to St. Louis and run that race, and then you can fix it up with God afterward.'

"And, well—friends, I did. I ran the race and won it, and then I came right back to Chicago, and went before the session of the church and owned up, and when they heard all about it they let me off, and I was an elder of that church for a good many years afterward. I have been sorry a thousand times since that I did this, but with my inexperience at that time, I could see no other way out of it."

One Sunday afternoon Billy was strolling about in the south end of the business district of Chicago, with half a dozen baseball friends. The New York Giants were in the city at the time, and several of them were in the party.

At the corner of State and Van Buren streets was an empty lot, which is now occupied by the Siegel & Cooper Department Store. Here a company of men and women workers from the Pacific Garden Mission were holding an outdoor meeting.

Sunday and his friends stopped to listen. The meeting soon took hold of their attention, and they sat down on the curb and heard the service through. Sunday confesses that the singing of the old gospel songs—the same his mother had sung in the little log cabin home back in Iowa—caught at his heart strings and set them vibrating in sympathy with memories of childhood days. A new spirit welled up within him, and created dissatisfaction with the life he was living.

When the outdoor meeting was over, a young man named Harry Monroe, now superintendent of the Mission, seeing that Sunday had been touched, went to him and invited him to attend the meeting at the Mission, two blocks away.

"You'll enjoy it," he said. "You'll hear some things that will interest you. Won't you come?"

Sunday accepted the invitation and went. The usual services were held in the Mission. There was singing and praying, and earnest and heartfelt testimonies from those who had found deliverance from many kinds of sin. Then some one gave a short gospel talk, that, though brief, was right to the point. The usual invitation to accept Christ was given, for no meeting has ever been held in that Mission without this being done, and there has never been a service when some one did not respond.

Sunday listened eagerly and closely to everything that was said, and though his heart was deeply stirred, he did not respond to the invitation, or in any way further commit himself; though when he left the Mission it was with the resolve that he would return again.

Several nights later he was once more in the Mission,

and went again some four or five nights in succession. Then one night when he needed help as badly as did the man at the pool of Bethesda, a voice that was like a breath from heaven aroused him, and he looked up into the face of Mrs. Clark, wife of the saintly Col. Clark, founder of the Mission. She well understood his case, for she had helped hundreds like him into the kingdom.

She talked to him like a mother, and with a wisdom given to her from above led him to where he could see the light streaming from the cross. Little by little she brought him to see clearly that eternal life is God's free gift, and being such, it must be received as a gift, through childlike faith in the finished work of Christ. And then, when the good woman had given him a few promises, upon which she assured him it would be safe to plant his feet, he made the great decision that every one must make for himself, and took Jesus Christ as his all-sufficient Saviour, promised compliance with all that God's law required of him, and then soon—very soon— his burden was gone. He knew that his name had been written in the Book of Life, and the peace that passeth understanding came into his heart.

The founder of the Pacific Garden Mission, in which Sunday was converted, was Col. Clark, who, when he was converted, was a Board of Trade man in Chicago, doing a very large and profitable business. This he gave up almost at once, and consecrated himself and all that he had to the work of God. As soon as the Holy Spirit took possession of his heart he became a most compassionate man, and could not look upon the unfortunate and sinful without being moved to tears. He was often seen by some passing friend, back in an alley, fifteen or twenty feet from the sidewalk, talking and praying with a man who had been torn by the cloven hoof, the tears on both their faces.

Soon Col. Clark began to cry to God almost constantly, to help him do something for the down-and-out people with whom he soon began to be brought much in contact. This resulted, not long after his conversion, in his starting the Pacific Garden Mission, which has from that day to this been a life-saving station for those whose lives have been wrecked by misfortune and sin.

A meeting has been held in this Mission every night for about forty years, and not one has ever been held in which some poor soul did not confess Christ and make a new start. Col. Clark put in six nights out of every week at the Mission as long as he lived, and often expressed the hope that he might be found there doing his duty when the Lord comes again. He could not preach at all, and was not much of a talker, but only the most hardened sinner could hear him pray and remain unmoved.

But think of the great harvest of good that came out of the life this gentle and unassuming man invested for God. It was in the Mission he founded and for many years supported, that Harry Monroe, its present able superintendent, was converted; here Melvin Trotter and others who have distinguished themselves as Mission workers, were converted, and it was here that Billy Sunday, one of the greatest evangelists since Pentecost, was converted, and yet while he lived it was given to Col. Clark to know very little about the real magnitude of his work. What encouragement this should be to each one of us, to be " always abounding in the work of the Lord, forasmuch as we know that our labor is not in vain."

Every morning the White Stocking boys went to the

Ball Park for practice. After his conversion Sunday went to the Park expecting to be greeted with ridicule, because of the stand he had taken for Christ. In one of his sermons he thus tells what happened:

"I shall never forget it! I slipped my key into the wicket, and the first to meet me after I got inside was Mike Kelly. He came up, and in a most cordial and brotherly manner said:

"'Bill, I'm proud of you. Religion ain't my long suit, but I'll help you all I can.'

"Up came Anson, the best ball player ever in the game; and after him Pfeffer, Clarkson, Flint, Jimmy McCormick, Burns, Williamson and Dalrymple. There wasn't a fellow in that team who knocked; but every one had a word of encouragement for me.

"Not long afterward we played the old Detroit team. We were neck and neck for the championship, and four games were going to settle it. That club had Thompson, Richardson, Rowe, Dunlap, Hanlon and Bennett, and they could play ball!

"I was playing right field. Mike Kelly was catching and John G. Clarkson was pitching. He was as fine a pitcher as ever crawled into a uniform. I think he could put more turns and twists into a ball than any pitcher I ever saw. There are some fine pitchers to-day —Bender, Wood, Matthewson, Johnson, Marquard and others, but I don't believe any of them stands in the class with Clarkson.

"They had two men out, and they had a man on second and another on third, with Bennett, their old catcher, at the bat. Charley had three balls and two strikes on him. He couldn't hit a high ball, but he could kill them when they went about his knee. I called to Clarkson, and said:

" ' One more, John, and we've got 'em! '

" You know every pitcher digs a hole in the ground where he puts his foot when he is pitching. John stuck his foot into the hole, and he went clear back to the ground. O how he could make them dance! He could throw overhanded and the ball would go down and up. He is the only man I ever saw do it. He could send a ball so swift that the batter would feel the thermometer drop as it whizzed by.

" John went clear down, and just as he let the ball go his right foot slipped, and the ball went low instead of high.

" I saw Charley swing hard, and heard the bat crack as he met the ball square on the nose. As I saw the ball rise in the air I knew it was going clear over my head, into the crowd that overflowed into the field. I could judge within ten feet of where a ball would light, so I turned my back to the ball and ran, and as I ran I yelled—

" ' Get out of the way! '

" And that crowd opened like the Red Sea for the rod of Moses. I ran on and as I flew over the dirt I made a prayer. It wasn't theological either, I tell you that. As near as I can remember, it was something like this:

" ' O Lord, if you ever helped mortal man, help me to get that ball! '

" I ran and jumped over the bench when I thought I was under it, and stopped. I looked back and saw it going over my head, and I jumped and shoved my left hand out, and the ball hit it and stuck! At the rate I was going the momentum carried me on, and I fell under the feet of a team of horses. But I held to it and jumped up with the ball in my hand. My! how they yelled! Tom

Johnson, who used to be mayor of Cleveland—dead now
—rushed up to me and poked a ten-dollar bill in my
hand.

" ' Here, Bill! ' he cried to me. ' Greatest thing I ever
saw! Buy yourself the best hat in Chicago on me! ' "

When A. G. Spalding got together the two famous
baseball nines which made a trip around the world, playing exhibition games in the big cities of a dozen coun-
tries, Sunday was the second man asked to join, and
Anson was the first. Just before they got started on the
trip, Sunday got hurt. He always slid head first for a
base, and in doing so cut a ligament loose in his knee.
He consulted a Washington, D. C., physician, and the
latter promised him a good sound leg if he would not
make the trip around the world.

It was a tremendous disappointment to the young
player, but he took the doctor's advice, and stayed at
home. Spalding offered to wait for him in either Hono-
lulu or Australia, and later sought to persuade him to
go over to England and play there and in Scotland and
Wales, but Sunday did not go.

Billy has always been grateful to the physician, who
was Dr. McGruder, Garfield's family doctor, for his firm
stand against the world tour. The restoration was perfect, and the knee to-day is as good as it ever was.

IV

AN ACTIVE MEMBER OF A LIVE CHURCH

SOON after Mr. Sunday's conversion he became a member of the Jefferson Park Presbyterian Church, of Chicago, located on the West Side, and was soon known as an energetic young man who was very much in earnest in his religious life.

That he should have become a most earnest Christian worker soon after his conversion is not surprising, for with his nature he could not long remain inactive in anything in which he took an interest. He must be up and doing in a way that will bring something to pass wherever he is. Even to this day when he goes home to rest, he gets into a suit of old clothes almost as soon as he takes off his hat, and out he goes to sprinkle the lawn, trim the shrubbery, dig in the ground or push the lawnmower. If he had to sit down and remain inactive for a day he would almost die of fatigue.

When Sunday came into the kingdom he had great love for the things of God, and especially so for the house of God and the people of God. The new nature, implanted when he was born from above, made the pleasures of the old life distasteful. Newer and more wholesome attractions supplanted them, and drew him away from the old entanglements.

From the very start he loved the Bible, and found in it a rich mine of golden treasure, in the seeking of which he spent many hours in fascinating interest. Then what more natural than that he should often be drawn to the place where the Book was honored, loved, obeyed and expounded? His first Bible was one he bought at a second-hand bookstore in St. Louis for thirty-five cents, and some of the most wonderful hours of his life were spent in poring over its pages.

When he became a Christian the highest mark of discipleship was not wanting in him, for he loved the brethren, and it became as natural for him to go to church as it is for birds to sing or flowers to bloom. Having fellowship with the people who knew the Lord, and never tired of telling of his goodness, gave him strength and courage, and joy of a higher order than he had ever before known.

He became a regular attendant upon all the church services whenever he was in the city, and it was not long before he began to take some part in them. He loved to pray, and has never gotten over this life-giving habit. Prayer was to him the natural expression of the worship that welled up in his soul, and it is not surprising that he was soon praying in public. He prayed because his heart was full of praise that could not be suppressed. It had to find vent in glad expression, just as all nature must burst into bud when spring comes. And so, whenever there was an opportunity to pray in the devotional meetings, others might hold back, but the young convert could not; and when he prayed all who heard knew that it was real prayer that he offered. He not only thanked God for what had been given, but put out his hands for more, in a way that left no doubt that he expected them to be filled.

There was this beautiful thing too about his prayers; they were natural. There was nothing strained or worked up in them. They poured out with no more

evidence of artificiality than water bubbling out of a
spring. They were not modeled after the conventional
pattern, and never have been, any more than the prattle
of a child conforms to the rules of rhetoric.

Sunday could not be put in a more uncomfortable
strait-jacket than to have to pray in a dignified and
perfectly proper manner. Whatever he does he must
do in his own natural way, and that explains why he is
Billy Sunday. He is natural. He does his best in a
way that is as much according to his nature as the color
of his eyes; and this practice, this scorn of pretense, is
one of the reasons why he is to-day a mighty man for
God. He is as certain that God hears him when he
prays as he is that he lives. Without prayer he believes
that he would be as quickly shorn of his strength as
Samson was. He therefore takes no step and makes
no decision without first laying the matter before the
Lord. His prayers are not long, but he puts them close
together, and so keeps close to God in his every-day life,
for it is his habit to pray about the little things as well
as the great ones. His praying, like everything else he
does, is quite unconventional.

When Sunday prays he talks to the Lord, as to his
most intimate friend, and seldom uses the words " thee "
and " thou." More frequently he begins by saying, " And
now, Jesus," and then comes at once to the matter of
the moment, without preamble or circumlocution. In
this way he not only prays for guidance as to the sermon
he shall preach, and that it may be delivered with power,
and other matters pertaining to the success of the meeting, but prays for good order and good weather as
well.

In every place where he holds a meeting he chooses
some secluded spot, where he can spend a few minutes in

prayer before he enters the tabernacle, and this spot becomes a bethel to him.

He also believes that power will come, and all difficulties, however great, will be swept away when a great stream of united prayer is kept going up to heaven, and so in every neighborhood of six or eight blocks, cottage prayer meetings are held every day, at the same hour, and changed from home to home each morning.

But to go back to the beginning of his church life. In that early day he was as ready to testify to what had been done for him and in him as was the blind man in the ninth chapter of John. The moment the meeting was open for testimony the young convert was on his feet, and the spiritual temperature was always somewhat higher when he closed than when he began, for he always had something to say that was fresh and crisp, and worth the telling. This was largely because he had become such a diligent reader of the Bible. And whenever he spoke it was with an enthusiasm that was contagious, and this had a retroactive effect upon his own heart that greatly helped his spiritual development and growth.

And how richly God rewarded the young convert for his unwavering and determined stand from the very beginning of his religious life. The promises of the first psalm were fulfilled to him and in him, for like a tree planted by the rivers of water, everything he said and did was made to prosper in a rich fruitage of Christian character. In the prayer meetings he met those of kindred spirit, and with them had a fellowship like to that above. In his church life he shirked no duty that was laid upon him, and for a time was a faithful superintendent of the Sabbath school.

He joined the Central Y. M. C. A. Bible Training

Class, and learned to study the Scriptures systematically. This was of lasting benefit to him, and no doubt has had much to do with causing him to make systematic Bible study a prominent feature of his great meetings.

Being in attendance upon the services in a church in Allegheny, Pa., one Sunday, he was asked to serve as teacher to a class of young men, in the Sunday school, and with his usual promptness cheerfully responded. The young fellows in the class were much pleased with this arrangement, and began at once to ply him with all sorts of baseball questions. Sunday at once stopped and said:

" Fellows, if you'll come around to the hotel where I am stopping, to-morrow, I will be glad to tell you all I can about baseball, but I can't do it to-day. This is God's day, and I am here to do his work the best I know how, and so let us see what we can get out of this lesson."

There was no further interruption, and every young man in the class listened attentively to all that was said. Some time ago a gray-haired usher in one of Sunday's great meetings recalled the scene to his recollection, and told how deeply he had been impressed by the tactful way in which the young teacher had handled the matter.

Sunday continued to play ball as a professional for about five years after his conversion, but while doing so was unconsciously making a splendid preparation for preaching, by giving religious talks as he had opportunity in cities to which he traveled with his club. In those days he had not the slightest thought of ever becoming a preacher. The first doors that opened to him were those of Young Men's Christian Associations, but it was not long before churches also began to give him urgent calls to speak in their pulpits.

SQUIRE MARTIN COREY, MR. SUNDAY'S GRANDFATHER.

A Chicago paper has this to say about his first appearance as a speaker at a religious meeting in that city:

"Center fielder Billy Sunday made a three-base hit at Farwell Hall last night. There is no other way to express the success of his first appearance as an evangelist in Chicago. His audience was made up of about five hundred men, who didn't know much about his talents as a preacher, but could remember his galloping to second base with his cap in his hand.

"His talk was the most successful given in Farwell Hall for a year. He aimed straight at the young men in front of him, giving the truth in plain earnest language, and when he finished forty-eight of them raised their hands as seekers. After the regular service an inquiry meeting was held, in which Sunday took an active part, praying for and talking with the inquirers."

About the same time a New York paper had this to say of him there:

"If W. A. Sunday plays ball as well and as earnestly as he talked yesterday before a large body of young men in the hall of the Young Men's Christian Association, he ought to be in great demand among the rival clubs. Although athletic young men were especially invited to hear the ball player, not many were present who were known to be devoted to either professional or amateur athletics, but for all that the audience was a large one. The address was on 'Earnestness in Christian Work,' and it was delivered in a way that was in full harmony with the subject.

"'I love to see a man in earnest in everything he does,' said the speaker, 'and God has no use for a milk-and-water man. To succeed in business, in a profession or in athletics, you have got to be in earnest. You must never be discouraged, no matter what comes, for no man ever climbed a mountain who was scared dizzy at the sight of a molehill. So in your lives as Christians, you must put your whole heart in whatever you undertake, and always move onward and upward with spirit.'

" Mr. Sunday spoke fluently and with great feeling, and the many who followed him into the inquiry meeting, to which he invited them, showed that his words had been with telling effect."

It will be noticed that in his very first efforts Sunday always had results, and this seems to have been because in his preaching he aimed for them and expected them. This is still characteristic of him, for he never begins a campaign without believing that thousands will be converted, and in final results his forecasts are always more than fulfilled. No matter how well the sermon may sound, if the preacher expects nothing he is not likely to be surprised. To shoot without aim is a waste of powder.

Another eastern paper gave this graphic picture of one of Sunday's early efforts in the pulpit:

" It is something of a novelty to see a professional ball player get up in the pulpit, and forgetting base hits, home runs, brilliant catches and the plaudits of the big throng for awhile, expound the great doctrines of Christ in such a pathetic and forcible manner as to almost bring tears to the eyes of over fifteen hundred people. Yet that is the novelty that was presented to the First Presbyterian Church of Manayunk last night, and the gentleman whose eloquence astonished the assembly was William A. Sunday, the center fielder of the Philadelphia (N. L.) Baseball Club. It was a revelation to most of those who were present. He directed the force of his address to young people in general, and to young men in particular. He based what he had to say on Psalm 116: 12-13.

"'No matter what may be their standing in life, whether rich or poor, high or low, moral or immoral, all young people have their temptations,' he began, 'and those who do not yield to them in a greater or lesser degree are few and far between. Those who are really bad in mind, and are not reached by the Christianizing influences of the Church of God, take these temptations as they come to them and yield, scarcely knowing that they do, and by so doing get farther and farther from where the grace of God can affect them. Those whose moral tendencies are in the direction of moral and upright life, recognize the temptation when it comes and resist it. The way, therefore, to be fortified and strengthened to meet temptations as they come, is to get within the fold of the Church, where you can look to God for help and protection against all evil.'

"Many were visibly affected by the clearness and earnestness with which the layman addressed them, in a voice of tender pleading, and urged them to make the decision and take the step that would make them safe."

This also from a Pittsburg paper, concerning one of his very early efforts, as any one who has heard him in recent years can tell at a glance:

"As a public speaker, William A. Sunday, more familiarly known on the diamond as 'Billy,' can compare favorably with a majority of young clergymen in the city pulpits. He is not an ordained minister, but a member of the Pittsburg Baseball team, with Christian principles. When speaking, his delivery is pleasant and grammatical. He has a ready command of the English language, and uses many poetic phrases. His knowledge of human nature and the Scriptures were clearly evident in the half-hour's address at the Young Men's Christian Association yesterday afternoon. He made no reference to the baseball profession, and instead of using slang, his words were well chosen. He spoke earnestly, but at first seemed somewhat nervous. As he warmed up to his subject he overcame his uneasiness. His gestures were in harmony with his words, and his sentences complete and well rounded. There was an attendance of about eight hundred, all young men, who were much interested in the address."

After becoming a professional baseball player, Sunday was engaged by the athletic associations of Northwestern University, in Evanston, to spend his winters there and coach the baseball teams in their preliminary training. There again he improved his time by taking special studies in the University. He was deeply interested in the study of English, rhetoric and relative branches. The knowledge he there gained of history shows in his preaching to-day. He did good work in physiology and greatly liked anything geographical. He had no turn for mathematics, and yet knowing their great importance, compelled himself to dig into them, and often to-day fairly amazes his great congregations by the way he piles up figures. What Sunday did at Northwestern, coupled with what he has been doing ever since in self-culture, has given him a fine education. He never holds a meeting without creating astonishment at the extent and wide range of his information. He also has the rare gift of being able to inform others in a way that charms them into giving the closest attention. Even the dry bones of statistics seem to live and breathe under his magic touch.

It seems incredible, but he can spend five minutes in describing the eye of a fly, in a way so graphic, and yet so telling and simple, that those who hear almost hold their breath lest they miss a word. And yet this is the man that poorly informed newspapers, at a distance from where he preaches, declare to be "ignorant and uncouth."

Many of the top-heavy Pharisees no doubt believed that John the Baptist didn't know enough to go in out of the rain, because his phylacteries were not broad and loaded with starch like their own.

While a student at Northwestern, Sunday was a classmate of Clem Studebaker, Jr., and E. J. Ridgway, now editor of *Everybody's Magazine*. Prof. Charles Curtiss, now Dean of the Agricultural College at Ames, Iowa, was also a classmate in the high school at Nevada.

Even in his early boyhood schooldays Sunday was a good speaker, and had the knack of getting and holding attention, for his dynamic energy and intense earnestness, in connection with his strong dramatic talent, made his declamatory efforts vastly different from the average schoolboy recitation in singsong. He put the same kind of life and reality into them that he did into playing ball and leapfrog, and that is why there was always a flutter of expectation among the boys and girls when it was known that Willie Sunday was going to "speak a piece."

Had Billy been born in an Indian tribe he would probably have been called "Eagle Eye," for he can see like a bird. He has a vision so keen that he can clearly see the face of the most distant person in his largest audiences, and this, as every speaker knows, has been an advantage of great importance to him.

His good eyesight has also quite naturally made him a keen and close observer, so that wherever he goes he almost unconsciously finds and stores away for future

use good material for illustrations and sermons, as a be
stores up honey. He will walk quickly through a room
a large railway station or a factory without appearin
to notice anything, and yet will afterward, when leas
expected, describe all that was in sight. Had he take
up the career of a detective he might have made Sherlocl
Holmes look to his laurels.

Sunday is also a great student of human nature an
a close observer of character. He is seldom mistake
in his estimate of a person, and seems never to forge
a face he has once seen. When he begins a new meetin
it is surprising in what a short time he will know al
the ministers and ushers by name, and be almost a
well posted concerning the business men, city and count
officials, school teachers and others, as a local politicia
He also quickly absorbs and assimilates information a
to local affairs, and before being on the scene a wee
will be posted like a native.

Among his other experiences, Sunday was for a tim
a fireman on the railroad. This has given him a stron
hold on railroad men, so that in every railroad tow
where he has held meetings—and they have been many—
he has had many converts among them. In shop talk
to them he can talk so glibly about " filing brasses,
" gumming out nozzles," " leaky flues," " broken side
rods " and " blown-out cylinder heads " that through th
freemasonry of the rail every man of them knows tha
Billy has been there.

In the meeting at Burlington, Iowa, more than a sco
of engineers were converted, and the same was also th
case at Austin, Minn. There was a time when abo
every man who drove a fast train on the Burlingto
between Chicago and Omaha had been converted in
Billy Sunday meeting. The railroad men all seem t

AT THE AGE OF 23.   AT THE AGE OF 24.

AT THE AGE OF 25.   AT THE AGE OF 30.

know him and love him, and he is sure of finding warm friends among them wherever he goes. Unless he is greatly pressed for time, he seldom leaves a train on which he has traveled any distance without making his way to the cab to have a few words with the engineer.

V

PLAYING BALL AND GIVING RELIGIOUS TALKS

IT was certainly not a matter of mere chance that Sunday's first religious talks were given for Young Men's Christian Associations. In no other part of his career is it more evident that he was clearly directed by the hand of God. His first calls coming from the source they did, made it inevitable that his first audiences should be composed mainly of young men, and this undoubtedly decided the character of his preaching and evangelism.

There is nothing more natural than for a speaker to adapt what he says to the needs and understanding of those to whom he speaks, and this perhaps, more than anything else, had to do with making Sunday a preacher to men and a winner of men, for by this characteristic he has from the outset been distinguished.

He preaches a stalwart gospel that appeals to men, attracts men to hear it, and in a way little short of marvelous. It is doubtful if any evangelist since the day of John the Baptist has been so unmistakably a preacher to men as William A. Sunday. Among his converts, wherever he goes, are hundreds and thousands of men. His men's meetings have been, without a chance for doubt, the largest ever held anywhere, and among those who take a stand in them are men of every grade known in the community, from the humblest to the highest. This is because he learned right at the beginning to preach with a definite object in view, and with a confidence that results would be exactly what he aimed for.

Had his first converts been made up of people of all kinds and conditions, it is not certain that he would so soon have learned to draw a bead in his preaching, but seeing so many young men before him, he would instinctively try to reach young men with his message. Being himself a young man, he knew young men, and he knew what their sins and temptations were. He knew what pitfalls were set for their undoing, and thundered out warnings against them in a way that was tremendously effective. He gave no heed to glittering generalities, but loaded up with buckshot and tried to shoot to kill. The rough old flintlock he took up and began to load and fire, was not as elegant as the nickel-plated capsnapper that is so often sent out from the homiletic arsenal, but every time he pulled the trigger big game was sure to fall.

An examination of Sunday's earliest efforts shows that he always sought to hit the nail squarely on the head, and to hit it hard when the blow fell. He didn't fire loud broadsides into the sins of people on the other side of the world, as many well-meaning preachers sometimes do, but he took a dead aim at the vices and misdoings of the young fellow who sat there before him, and that is why he has always made the feathers fly.

When he saw the young fellows look scared and turn pale, he knew he was beginning to draw blood, and so he would lower his aim a little, and then let them have it again right where they lived. There may perhaps be a preacher here and there who could preach for years in a community where every man always stole the chicken for his Sunday dinner, and yet never put anything in a sermon that would throw a chill over the meeting, but it couldn't be that way with Billy Sunday.

The man who feels a proud complacency in thinking how much better he is than other men is certain to begin to squirm very soon after he comes under Sunday's preaching, and all because Billy has learned so well how to fire the shot and shell of gospel truth as to make it hit about everything under the sun that bears the name of sin.

No doubt the ex-ball player's experience on the diamond has had much to do with making him always have a clear and definite purpose in view every time he takes a text. As a ball player, he had soon learned that no ball was ever to be thrown just to keep it in motion, but that it should go with a true aim whenever it left the hand.

As a ball player, it had been his habit to try to send the ball right where it ought to go to hurt the other side and help his own—and do it quick. And so it may be that to his athletic training is due some of the earnestness and precision with which he preaches. At all events, it is certainly true that he goes to the pulpit with as strong a determination to win there as he carried with him to the diamond.

In the early days men flocked to hear Sunday because they knew how well he could play ball, and they probably reasoned that the man who would do that so well would not preach poorly, and in this they were not mistaken. They knew there was always something doing when the ball was batted his way or when it was time for him to go to the plate.

A stolen base by him often stirred up the fans more than a home run by another player. They had seen

SUNDAY IN HIS OLD NATIONAL LEAGUE UNIFORM.

games played in which he had been the only man to make a run, and they believed there would be something doing that would be well worth seeing and hearing when he stepped into the pulpit. So from the very beginning the audiences he drew were large, and from that day to this he has never held a meeting in a building that was large enough to accommodate the crowds he drew.

Sunday was not only clear and pointed in his first preaching, but was also practical. No man could hear him without learning something that would help him toward a better life, and whatever he said was also characterized by good common sense. When he hitched his wagon to a star he was careful to keep all the wheels on the ground. He ran off at no tangents, but stayed in the middle of the road.

There was nothing wishy-washy or theologically nonsensical even in his earliest declarations. From the beginning he insisted that there could be no salvation for any kind of a sinner without true repentance from all sin and faith in Jesus Christ. The keynote of his preaching, then as now, was that without Christ no man is saved, and with him no one is lost.

From the beginning his preaching was full of originality, and intensely interesting. There was a charm and freshness about it that was a constant surprise. The common people flocked to hear him because they could understand him. No matter what his subject chanced to be, he made the points stick out like the ears of a rabbit. And this is still true of him. Not once in a meeting does he ever lose his freshness or vigor. The demand for seats at the close of a meeting is, if anything, stronger than at the beginning. He is never monotonous, but is as full of variety as a kaleidoscope.

In handling themes in which it is difficult to interest

an ordinary mind, Sunday surprises and delights. He will take an old subject, and by a few unexpected touches make it new. In his hands a Bible incident will seem to be something you have seen with your own eyes. He will make the Roman centurion almost take you by the hand, and begin to tell you all about the part he had in the seventh chapter of Luke.

When blind Bartimeus receives his sight you could not be any more glad to have the same thing happen with your own brother, and you will rub your eyes and almost believe you can see Zaccheus climbing the tree, and when he takes the Master and his disciples home with him, you witness the whole scene. It is not a recitation to you, but the real thing.

Being richly endowed with a creative imagination and rare descriptive power, Sunday can take an abstract statement of fact, that to the common mind will seem to be scarcely more than a dry bundle of bones, and in the twinkling of an eye it will become a thing of life, and that is why the multitudes will hang on his lips day after day, for many weeks, without any abatement of interest.

And that is why it would be a good thing for every preacher within a hundred miles of a Sunday meeting to go and hear a few sermons as a part of his postgraduate course in practical homiletics. He may have his clerical dignity rumpled somewhat, but he will learn how to get closer to men.

The *Advance* had this to say of Sunday quite recently:

" Let us consider him as a phenomenon before we consider him as an evangelist, and thus avoid, if possible, the divided feeling regarding evangelism.

" As a phenomenon we see him drawing amazing audiences, not only once or twice, or several times, but day and night for weeks. We see one throng trying to get into his big tabernacle before another gets out. We see all kinds of organizations of men asking for reservations in the building. We see trainloads of people coming from neighboring towns. And he is drawing all these multitudes just when magazine writers and critics of Christianity are declaring that the pulpit has lost its power. How many other men in America could attract such throngs week after week? Could any half-dozen of the best orators in the land put together do it?

"The eloquence of Webster and Clay is echoing in college halls and on political platforms, but did we ever hear that either of them kept tens of thousands of people coming to hear them through a period of six weeks, in the same place and on the same theme?

"And these people do not simply applaud and laugh and then go away. It is one thing for a political leader to awaken a deafening roar of applause. It is another thing to make men and women weep over sins, and promise to change their habits of life. With all his wonderful eloquence and mastery over multitudes, Webster could not master his own love for drink, but this man puts such a spell upon his fellowmen that they go away with so great a grip on their habits and appetites as to become new men. The very markets have to change their orders after Billy Sunday has been in town.

"We say, therefore, that William A. Sunday is as remarkable a human phenomenon as can be found in the land.

"In the next place, let us consider this man as a preacher. He is not exactly eloquent and not at all elegant. He says he is 'scared' of dignity, and dignity would be equally frightened if it met him out alone. Both do well to go armed when in the same vicinity.

After a fashion, he is a preacher from the wilderness, and his messages are clothed in camel's hair, goatskins and sheepskins, hide, hoof, horns and all. And when some of his most excited denunciations are over there is a smell of a volcano in the air. He uses the word hell so freely and frequently that it seems like a pet in the household of his vocabulary.

" And yet the people nearly fall over one another in the rush and crush to hear him. They come in automobiles, in trains, on foot, and when there they camp down and wait for hours until he ' goes to the bat.'

" How shall we explain it? Is it because this preacher who graduated from the ball ground to the pulpit uses language which the people better understand than they do the cultured speech of the graduate? In parting with dignity, did Mr. Sunday become hale fellow well met with men who live in the market place six days in the week and go to church on one day? Is it because he tells a story in the same language that the story-teller in the corner grocery uses, that he ' gets next ' to the average man?

" We do not answer these questions, but we do say that if we were trying to teach men how to preach we should make a study of Mr. Sunday and his meetings. A great United States Senator followed Col. Ingersoll all over the state of Maine to hear him captivate the crowds in a great political campaign. It would be well if some theological professor followed Billy Sunday long enough to get hold of the psychology of his success in attracting multitudes.

" In closing, let us consider in a brief word the fact that the message of this man is that of the prophets, priests and preachers of the ages. Could he hold the multitudes with any other message? Certainly not. Let men say what they will about religion being played out, it still is the one thing that gets nearer to the center of human interest than any other theme. The very faults of Mr. Sunday's preaching, about which his critics so severely complain, should help to convince them, and all of us, that the American people are still in the grip of a profound belief in God."

VI

MEETS HIS FUTURE WIFE AT A PRAYER MEETING

IT is very significant that Sunday first met the woman who became his wife at a prayer meeting, a pretty sure evidence that the hand of the Lord had much to do with arranging a life partnership for the man who was to be so wondrously used as an evangelist.

Among the members of the church with which he united was a young woman by the name of Helen A. Thompson, a deeply religious young lady, who was a Sunday school teacher and an active worker in the Christian Endeavor Society. She had for about six years been living a devoted and consecrated Christian life. and was exerting a constantly widening influence for good.

She was also a young woman of strong personality, artistic temperament and unmistakable talent in several lines, not the least of which was her rare good sense. She was of a nature so ardent and ingenuous that religion with her had to be a life, and for life, and this was the young woman in whose acquaintance with Mr. Sunday the hand of the Lord is as clearly seen as it was in leading the servant of Abraham to find a bride for Isaac in Rebecca.

Miss Thompson's father was William Thompson, one of the pioneer wholesale dairymen and ice cream manufacturers of Chicago. He was a soldier in the Civil

War, and was badly wounded at the battle of Shiloh. He served in Company I, Fifty-second Illinois Infantry. He was converted after he had passed the meridian of life, and had united with the same church Mr. Sunday joined, and continued in that relation until his death.

Mrs. Sunday's mother died several years ago. As may be supposed, from the way in which she trained her daughter, she was a woman of sterling Christian character. Both of Mrs. Sunday's parents were of old Scottish stock, and were born in the Highlands. She is very proud of her Scottish ancestry, and rejoices in the fact that she is a full-blooded Scot. She was born at Dundee, Ill.

When Sunday and Miss Thompson first met it was a case of love at first sight with him, but not so with her. She already had a friend toward whom she had quite a strong inclination. Soon after she and Sunday began to meet in church circles, she tried to get him interested in one of her girl friends, and so managed as to have them frequently thrown together, but beyond this all her scheming failed.

But finally Sunday managed in some way to get the girl by whom he had been so deeply smitten to see that he had no interest at all in her chum, but did have a great interest in her.

It was some time, however, before the course of his wooing became anything like smooth, and mainly because Mr. Thompson brought down his foot against his daughter having a ball player for a suitor, though Mrs. Thompson was very much predisposed in his favor because he was a Christian.

While this state of affairs existed he could not call upon the young woman at her home. The only place he could make sure of seeing her was at the prayer meeting; but then her 'steady company' was there too. This rival took her home week after week, but Billy bided his time, and at last there came a time when Helen was there alone. He was quick to improve his opportunity and was accepted as an escort.

The Thompson home was only a hundred yards from the church, but the very first shot out of the box the ball player inaugurated a new system—for he was a 'fielder' and no 'short-stop,' and so he insisted upon walking around four sides of the block to the Thompson home, instead of half of one. From that time on he had his innings, and was never whitewashed.

Sunday was twenty-four years old when he met his future wife. He had been playing with the Chicago White Stockings since 1883. Her home was at the corner of Throop and Adams streets. The West Side Ball Grounds were between Harrison and Congress streets, and Billy managed to pass the Thompson home four times a day while the team was playing on the home grounds. Mrs. Sunday says the front steps seemed to need sweeping many times a day when the team was on the local schedule.

Many who were acquainted with the old West Side Ball Park in Chicago will remember the toboggan slide Anson had in operation there during favorable weather in the winter time. Anson was never more contented than when, for one reason or another, he had Sunday with him. His partiality for the young player had long been noted, but Sunday was so generally liked it had never caused any enmity or jealousy. So Anson insisted that Sunday should act as one of the managers of the slide, and to this Billy agreed on condition that Helen Thompson should have all the free slides she wanted. The number of these turned out to be many.

In the spring of 1888 Sunday was sold by the Chicago White Stockings to the Pittsburg team. This caused a great separation between the lovers that was most trying to them, but it added not a little to Uncle Sam's revenue from the sale of postage stamps.

"I frequently got letters from him that were forty-eight pages long," says Mrs. Sunday, "and really they contained nothing but variations of 'I'm so lonesome!'"

It may not be surprising to the reader to know that this lonesome feeling still troubles Mr. Sunday whenever he has to be separated from his wife.

There is one room in their home at Winona Lake in which Mrs. Sunday keeps a small old-fashioned sofa and a picture that hung over it in Father Thompson's parlor when the baseball player went there courting her. The picture was from her own easel, and one of her earliest efforts in the realm of art.

They were married September 5, 1888, and made their wedding journey in connection with the movements of the team at the close of the season.

Their marriage has been an ideal one, and though they have four children, two of whom are themselves married, the Sundays are still lovers, and never tire of each other's company. He never takes a step of any importance without consulting her; and there are not many minor affairs that he will decide without wanting to know what she thinks, and the moment he knows what she thinks he knows what he will do—and so does she. The same is no doubt just as true of her. Their married life is a partnership, in which each partner has equal rank in the firm, and an equal voice in all its transactions. She is the power behind the throne with him, and is just the kind of wife such a man must have to win a great success.

If the devil knows anything about the future, he must have been drugged and sound asleep when the young couple first met each other, or if he understands his business—and nobody better knows than Sunday that he does—it is hard to understand why he didn't take a hand in finding a wife for Billy, as he seems to have done for many preachers and evangelists, from Samson down to this morning's paper.

Everybody who knows Sunday knows that he has been made out of about the same kind of clay as that from which the Lord molded Simon Peter, with perhaps a little more sand, for he is impetuous, nervous and impulsive—saying and doing things to-day sometimes that he will be sorry for to-morrow. And just as a train that can eat up space at the rate of a mile or more a minute needs an airbrake able to ease it up when needed, so the dynamic William becomes a greater and more effective man by his life partnership with the cool-headed and far-seeing " Nellie."

Sunday's pent-up energy is so great that often he would go through a troop and leap over a wall, when it would be little more than a waste of muscle, were it not for the woman with the steady-going Scotch blood who stands beside him. Her Highland ancestry and Mac-Gregor training holds her steady and keeps her cool, collected and tactful under all circumstances, and the worth of this to the firm nobody more keenly appreciates and realizes than Sunday.

Sunday is always at his best when his wife is with him, and she so arranges matters at home that she can spend a great deal of time with him in every campaign, and is therefore a constant help and inspiration to him. She is not only a wise counselor and good in planning, but is a good evangelist herself, and is ready and qualified

OLD SOFA FROM THE THOMPSON HOME, "JUST BIG
ENOUGH FOR TWO."

to lend a hand wherever needed. He hates to have her away from him, even for a day, and when he goes to make a single address nearly always takes her along.

What a mighty influence, therefore, did Sunday's meeting with this woman, while his Christian life was in the formative period, have upon all his after career. We all know that he has done a great work—an immense work—but only God himself knows how great and far-reaching has been the work of the faithful woman who has stood by his side in every campaign.

VII

LEAVES BASEBALL TO ENGAGE IN RELI-
GIOUS WORK

I T has been shown that Sunday's first Christian work, outside of the church with which he had united, was in responding to calls for religious talks from Young Men's Christian Associations, and then a little later he had many opportunities to speak to young people in Sunday schools, Christian Endeavor Societies and in the churches, and by these efforts his talent for public speaking was being developed.

His first addresses having been given for Young Men's Christian Associations, naturally turned his attention more directly to the work they were doing, and having a great personal interest in them, and especially in young men, and believing that field to be one of the greatest and most promising for Christian effort, the conviction grew upon him that he ought to do what he could in connection with the Y. M. C. A. organization, just as Moody had been led to do at the beginning of his public religious career.

Several places in Association work had opened up to him, and the Central Association in Chicago, especially, had for some time been strongly urging him to become the Secretary of its Religious Department. This he was eager to do, although the pay was only eighty-three dollars per month, and he was receiving several hundred

for playing ball. But there seemed to be an insurmounta-
ble difficulty in the way, and that was a contract with
his baseball managers that still had several years to run.
He had asked to be released from this contract, but after
he became a Christian they seemed to be even more
anxious to keep him, on account of his good influence
over other players. Every man of them had a higher
respect for him, for the stand he had taken, and cut out
profanity and rough talk when with him.

But the Chicago Association continued to urge him
to accept the position it had offered, and he being so
strongly inclined to go into that work, could not but feel
that it must be of God, and so he began to earnestly
pray that the difficulty might be removed.

Previous to this time there had been a movement in
which many of the old National League players had with-
drawn from their teams, and established what was
known as the Brotherhood Association, the forerunner
of the American League. In the spring of 1891 the
Brotherhood players returned to the National League,
and this breakup of the Brotherhood came quite provi-
dential for Sunday, as it flooded the baseball market
with players, and his managers became willing to release
him.

Sunday at once accepted the position that had been
offered him by the Chicago Association, and filled it for
three years. Time after time the head of the Association work in Chicago sought to persuade him to take
charge of the physical culture and gymnastic work, but
his heart was in religious work and he could not think
of doing anything else.

As it fell upon Sunday to provide speakers for the
noonday prayer and other meetings held in Farwell
Hall, his connection with the Central Association brought

him in close touch with the ministers of the city, and made him acquainted with many visitors who were men of prominence in various religious bodies.

The experience Sunday had in Association work in Chicago has been of untold value to him since, for it brought him in contact with many people who needed all the help that God could give them. This greatly quickened his own faith, for he had many opportunities of seeing that God " is mighty to save, and strong to deliver." His duties often had much in them of a home missionary character. Visiting the sick and destitute, praying with the troubled, comforting the afflicted and burying the dead.

At one hour he might be going about among the saloons, distributing cards of invitation to meetings and urging those he found there to attend, while the next he might be on his knees praying for some despairing man who had just been making a fruitless attempt at suicide. One day the duty of the hour would be to lead the noonday prayer meeting at Farwell Hall, while on another it might be to go about among the business men, trying to raise money enough to save some poor mother with a brood of little children and a drunken husband from being set out on the street.

Could the busy man of whom we speak only take time to write out some of his recollections of heartbreaking experiences he witnessed when serving as Secretary of Religious Work with the Chicago Association, they would make a tale to melt a heart of stone. They would also help us to understand why from that time to this he has had such a great passion for souls that it has carried him on from meeting to meeting, and from one hard campaign to another, pouring out his life and strength without stint, and amazing his friends at the way he has managed to stand up under his burden with scarcely any rest.

It may also be that the strange and unexpected experiences he encountered on the dark side of the great city had no little to do with shaping the whole course and character of Sunday's after ministry, and especially so of his preaching. Going into places so low down in sin and degradation, and witnessing the effect the simple presentation of the Word of God could produce there, and the transforming wonders the Spirit of God could work there, would make the presence and power of God a reality to be safely relied upon ever afterward.

This would convince Sunday, as nothing else could, that nothing short of absolute regeneration could ever stop and heal the awful ravages of sin. To attempt reform in the black depths of the great city would be as useless as trying to purify the ocean by pouring into it a few gallons of spring water, and that may be why the heart of his preaching has been, not mere reformation, but " Get Right With God!" And this, too, may account for his having been such a diligent reader of the Bible that his sermons are fairly saturated with the great truths of the wonderful Book.

Sunday's first experience in direct evangelistic work was in association with Dr. J. Wilbur Chapman, who, next to Moody, was the most widely known American evangelist. While Sunday was with the Chicago Association Chapman's singer was Peter Bilhorn, and he and Sunday were warm friends. It was through Bilhorn that Chapman and Sunday became acquainted. Dr. C. was greatly impressed by Sunday's earnestness and unusual power in reaching and winning men. He needed an assistant, and believed that Sunday's help would be just what he ought to have, so he made the ball player a proposition, which he at length accepted.

Sunday at first acted as an advance man. He would go into the new field and make the preliminary arrangements. He would superintend the erection of the tent, when one was used, get a band of singers organized, and look after necessary details. He would begin the meeting and do the preaching for a few days, until Dr. Chapman arrived, and then afterward would hold auxiliary meetings in outlying churches. At noontime he would speak to the men in shops, factories and other places. Through his co-operating assistance in this way, interest in the central meeting would be awakened much sooner.

Many of the meetings were held in large tents, but not all of them. Sometimes the place visited would have a large hall or other suitable building that could be utilized. A systematic organization was always effected, and the hearty co-operation of churches enlisted. Special services were held for young people, for children, for men and for women, and every legitimate means used to arouse the religious interest of the entire community. The unmistakable power of printer's ink was acknowledged, and almost invariably the press gave positive help, by publishing intelligent reports of the meetings. As no two meetings were alike, something was learned in each one that would add to the efficiency and effectiveness of the next.

By this it will be seen in what a splendid school young Sunday found himself, and how the hand of God was leading and preparing him for the great work he was being divinely chosen to accomplish. Hour by hour and day by day he was being taught the great lessons he must learn before he could reach the place where he could count on results almost with the precision of mathematics, as he does to-day.

While with Dr. Chapman Sunday assisted in meetings in Paris, Ill., Peoria, Ill., Terre Haute, Ind., Evansville, Ind., Indianapolis, Ind., Richmond, Ind., Oskaloosa, Iowa, Troy, N. Y., Gault, Can., and Huntingdon, Pa.

An Evansville paper had this to say of the opening of the meeting there by Mr. Sunday:

"Evans Hall was packed full last night with an expectant audience, ready to see the result of the first of the Chapman meetings, which are now upon us. A choir of two hundred voices occupied seats upon the platform, and gave a song service, while on an extension platform in front were seated the city pastors and Mr. Sunday, who was the speaker of the evening.

"In his unconventional and original way of putting things he is unreportable. He goes straight to the point in a most practical way that is all his own, bringing out his points with telling illustrations, and clinching them with original sayings that keep you from forgetting.

"'The Bible is a commonsense Book,' he said, 'for it shows man where he stands. The fact that there is joy in heaven over a repentant sinner shows that it must be an awful thing to be lost. It also shows that heaven takes an interest in men, and there is great joy there whenever a sinner is saved, because they know how great his peril has been.'

"He closed with an earnest prayer, and then while the Christians stood with bowed heads, he invited those who wanted to be, to raise their hands. In response to this, hands were lifted all over the house, and an after meeting was held."

A local paper had this to say of the meeting at Paris, Ill.:

" The services at the Christian Church yesterday morning, and at the Presbyterian Church in the afternoon, were well attended. Mr. Sunday was the leader at both places. It is evident that his baseball energy has been transferred to his new calling, for he is so much in earnest that his vitality shows in every sentence.

" About eighteen hundred people came to the tent last night expecting to hear Dr. Chapman, but a wreck on the Vandalia delayed his arrival until after nine o'clock. Meantime his helper, Mr. Sunday, took charge of the service and held the fort. He had the attention of everybody, and at once demonstrated that he was quite as efficient with the Bible as with the bat. He based what he had to say on the story of the rich young man, as given in Mark 10: 17-22. He had come running to Jesus, and kneeling before him, said: ' What shall I do, that I may inherit eternal life? ' and then went sadly away, when his question was answered in such an unexpected way.

" ' We never know what a man is worth,' said Mr. Sunday, ' until after he has been tested. Those who have most of self-confidence are often the first to break down, as this young fellow did. The test proves the real strength of a man, for no man is any stronger than he is at his weakest point. There was nothing unreasonable about what was required of this rich young man. God goes halvers on nothing, but demands all.

" ' No girl would be willing to marry a young man who would only promise to give her a little of his love. She must have it all, and so it is with God. He must be loved with the whole heart. With an undivided heart, and right there is where the young moneybags in the lesson fell down. He cared more for his ducats than he did for Christ, and that is what lost him his soul.

MRS. W. A. SUNDAY.

God has every right to demand our very best. It would have been no harder for the young man to give up all he had than for Abraham to give up his friends, his home and his native land. Peter left his boat and fishing nets—all he had—to follow Christ, and every Christian worth his salt does the same, and so must you and I.

" ' Matthew left his place of business as a tax collector to follow Jesus, and he didn't have to be told the second time. All the disciples gave up their business, their homes—everything—to follow the Master. There were no regrets, and they made no excuses. Even Christ gave up his place in heaven, and all the glory he had there, to suffer for our sakes, and certainly we should not hesitate to give up everything for him.

" ' The thing that wrecked the young man was his unwillingness to surrender the thing that held him to the earth. He wanted to go to heaven, but didn't want to give up the world, and this, I fear, is just as true of some of you. It is a noble thing to seek to know God's will, as this young man did, but an awful sin to refuse to obey it.' "

One day when Sunday was at home between meetings, his little daughter Helen, who had but recently commenced going to school, said to him:

" Papa, let's go to bed and tell stories."

" I can't do it, Helen, for I have to go away," said he.

" Where are you going to, papa?"

" Well, I've got to go to Urbana, Ohio, and then to Troy, and then to Evansville, and after that to Richmond, and then to Indianapolis."

" Papa, you're the best friend I've got, and I don't want you to go away. Let's go to bed and tell stories."

" But I must go away, my dear, and if you will be a

nice little girl and not cry, I will get you a present," her father said, trying to console her.

"Will you get me a ring?"

"Yes, I'll get you a ring."

"With a set in it?"

"Yes, I'll get you a ring with a little blue set in it." And he did. He got her a very pretty ring with a little turquoise set.

"But maybe I'd like to have a new dress, papa."

"All right. You shall have a new dress. What kind of a dress do you want?"

"I believe I would like to have a dress with some blue in it."

"All right. You shall have it; if you will be a good girl, and not cry."

And he afterward did that very thing. He went to Carson, Pierie & Scott's, and got her a very pretty silk dress with a blue stripe in it, that made her dance with delight when she saw it. She wore it for a long time, and then gave it to a poor little girl, who wore it till it looked like a battleflag.

But as soon as she had her father's promise for the ring and the dress, little Helen looked very sober and said:

"Papa, I don't want a ring; I don't want a dress. I just want you. You're the best friend I've got. Stay at home with me, papa, and I won't never want anything but you!"

"And that is the way it should be with the Christian," says Mr. Sunday, when he tells this touching incident. "The greatest desire of our hearts should be for a constant sense of the presence of Him whom having not seen we love."

VIII

BEGINNING OF SUNDAY'S EVANGELISTIC CAREER

SUNDAY continued with Dr. Chapman for three years, and then, during the holidays of 1895-6, Dr. C. wired that he had agreed to return to the pastorate of his old church in Philadelphia. Almost the same day that he received this message, he also received a telegram from a little town in Iowa named Garner, asking him to conduct a ten days' meeting there. Sunday has never been able to learn what prompted the call from Garner. He didn't know anybody there, and does not think any one living there had ever heard him preach. The call coming so opportunely, however, satisfied him that it was of the Lord, and he wired his acceptance.

At that time he had never held a meeting alone, and only had eight sermons, which would in some way have to be extended to ten. At that time there were two little children at home to be cared for, Helen and George, and it required a good deal of courage to swing out alone. But Sunday hurried out to Garner, and held a good meeting in the little opera house. He had no singer with him, and the choir numbered only twenty. On the last day of the meeting they took up a collection for him which footed up sixty-eight dollars. Two churches had united in that meeting.

From that day to this Sunday has never in all his

evangelistic career lacked a call for a meeting. Immediately following the meeting at Garner came others at Sigourney, Iowa, and Pawnee City, Neb.

From his experience in so many meetings with Dr. Chapman Sunday derived great benefit. There was no single detail in a series of special meetings with which his recent experiences had not made him familiar, and whatever came up he mastered so thoroughly that he grasped the meaning of other parts of the work. To this clear and practical knowledge of the requirements of each department is to be traced the ease and precision with which he to-day directs the multiplied activities of a great religious campaign. Many who come in contact with the executive side of a Sunday evangelistic movement are startled at its complexity, yet marvel at the smoothness with which it operates.

For some time after going to Garner, the meetings held by Sunday were in small towns, beginning generally in the largest church building, and then when the interest outgrew it, going to the opera house or largest hall. Many of the first calls received were from Iowa, the state in which he was born.

Though the work grew gradually, it increased steadily, and this it has continued to do up to the present time. It was not long before the Sunday meetings in various places were definitely fixed months in advance. At the present time meetings are arranged for two years in advance regularly, and occasionally more than that. The date for a campaign in Steubenville, Ohio, had been set three years in advance. The calls for meetings are now so many that a large number must of necessity be declined, and the evangelist has no task more trying than the arrangement of his schedule of future engagements.

From the very beginning, Sunday has insisted that the churches of the community should unite before he would agree to conduct a campaign. He has held that unless the forces for good were united little progress could be made against the work of the devil.

As the work grew it served to draw the Protestant churches in various communities into closer fellowship. To secure this agreement on the part of all the churches to give up their regular services during the meeting, and stand shoulder to shoulder, was not in every case easy to do, but the wisdom of it has been clearly shown in every instance. Three hundred churches united for the campaign in Pittsburg, Pa. Eight hundred churches united in extending a call to Mr. Sunday for a campaign in Philadelphia.

Sunday has always opposed the showing up of results in figures, or any attempt at a statistical summary of his years of evangelism, but a comparison can be made of one feature of the meeting in Garner, and another at Columbus, Ohio, in 1913. When Sunday went to Garner for his first meeting he had eight sermons only at his command. At Columbus he preached ninety-three in the tabernacle, taking no account of the special talks and addresses given in dozens of other places during the meeting.

Early in his evangelistic work Sunday employed a singer, and from that time on the music has always been a prominent feature of the tabernacle services.

In view of the great work Sunday has accomplished, the comments on his early meetings, published in the local papers, are most interesting. Here is one concerning a meeting held at Dunlap, Iowa:

" Scores have heard the message as never before, and have set out to lead Christian lives. Never in the history of Dunlap has there been such a spiritual awakening among the people. The result is not only seen in the revival meetings, but it has reached the Sunday schools and Young People's meetings, where the attendance has been greatly increased. Also offices, homes and places of business, where profanity has been smothered and prayers are heard. Dancing and card playing are no longer treated as trivial affairs, and good morals and right living are now matters of public concern.

"Mr. Sunday leaves town to-day, but his influence will remain for years to come. No one can measure its magnitude. Who can say how much trouble and grief have been averted by his coming? He will ever hold a warm place in the hearts of our people, who will wish him Godspeed in the work before him. The editor of the *Missouri Valley News,* who spent Sunday here, has this to say of the meeting:

"'We have heard of revivals in which the entire community was stirred as one man, but never before witnessed such a Pentecost as that of yesterday. Mr. Sunday is a young man, of near thirty-five, a perfect specimen of healthy, vigorous manhood. Since we taught him in his youth, he has been an impetuous, vigorous advocate of whatever he believed, and this spirit characterizes all his work as an evangelist. So great is his endurance that he can preach three times a day through an entire series of meetings, hold several specials, make personal calls, talk with seekers, and show no trace of fatigue. He looks on his work as being divinely directed. He said in his sermon yesterday, with an earnestness no one could doubt, that he expected to continue his labors until Gabriel sounded his trumpet from the sky.

"'His first work in any town is to revive the professors of religion; then he makes every one of them

WILLIAM THOMPSON.   MRS. WILLIAM THOMPSON.

MRS. SUNDAY'S FATHER AND MOTHER.

an evangelist for the time being. He has a trained chorister, who trains a large local choir and leads the singing. Every meeting begins with a song service. Then follows one of his characteristic sermons, full of fiery, forcible facts, quaint with homely, convincing and illuminative illustrations. Then a prayer service. Then a call for seekers to rise or raise their hands. Then the personal workers go out into the audience and invite those interested to go forward, and meantime the choir is singing appropriate gospel songs. There is tumult in all this, yet a serious, earnest spirit that is most impressive fills the place.

"'The meeting last night was of this order. Following the regular service, the after meeting was more like a jubilee or community praise meeting. The people sang as if inspired. The invitation brought forward old and young, from all classes, and frequently, as some well-known citizen would go forward, a shout of glad joy would break forth from the congregation; then others would go forward until the altar space was filled. Around that altar families were united, enmities were forgotten, and as the throng sang, "When the roll is called up yonder, I'll be there!" it seemed as if nothing more remained but for the people to go on their way rejoicing; but there they stayed, and sang on. For over an hour the people filed past the newly blessed, giving greeting and good cheer. In perfect order the work went on, songs breaking out at intervals, as if the hearts of the multitude could not contain their joy.'"

Another of those early meetings was held at Emerson, Iowa, and here are some of the things the local paper had to say about it:

"Over a hundred were converted during the three weeks' meeting, and our little town has never witnessed such a transformation in its history. Mr. Sunday was listened to every night by an audience that packed the opera house to its utmost capacity at every service. Many a calloused and wicked heart has been changed, and many homes have been made happy. Prayer and Bible-study meetings have been organized, and are doing much good in encouraging and assisting the young Christians. The evangelist's power in holding the close attention of his audience all the way through is wonderful, and his resources seem to be boundless. His vivid imagination, irresistible humor and untiring earnestness make him an unusually interesting and most effective preacher.

"When Sunday went to take the train to leave us, it looked as if nearly all the town went to the depot to see him off. His hand was shaken by everybody who could get to him, and as the train started, hands and handkerchiefs were waved and gospel songs sung as long as the train could be seen. He will begin his next meeting at Malvern next Sunday, to which place the prayers of all Emerson will follow him, and there is no doubt but that many will go and lend a helping hand some time during his stay there."

The meeting at Malvern also continued three weeks, and was in every way a most successful one. In Sunday's early meetings the length of time covered by each was not over three weeks, for in those days his stock of sermons was by that time about used up, and yet the results secured in that brief time were generally most remarkable.

The Malvern paper had this to say of the meeting:

"Many misgivings and doubts were expressed by Christian people as to the expediency of having Mr. Sunday come here, based upon distorted and malicious reports as to his manner and methods. Practically all these prejudices had vanished before he had been here a week, and we do not believe he left the town bearing the ill will of a single person. From the start, almost, there was a general rallying of the church people about him, and as he fearlessly, yet lovingly proclaimed the plain truths of the gospel, the hearts of old and young were touched, and the desire for a higher and purer plane of living became general. During the meeting two hundred and thirty began a Christian life. There must have been fully a thousand people present at the closing service Sunday evening, and there were many others who could not squeeze into the church. The generous free-will offering of our people to Mr. Sunday footed up $675.

"This three weeks' series of meetings has been a marvelous one. In most respects, the most remarkable ever held in Mills county. The attendance during the entire three weeks, in spite of unpropitious weather, has been phenomenal. The meetings were held in the Baptist Church, which will accommodate about a thousand people, and it was filled every night to overflowing. There has been a remarkable improvement in Sunday's delivery, language and entire style of address since we heard him about three years ago. We are no prophet, but we predict it will be only a question of time when he will take rank with the greatest evangelists in the country."

Here are a few lines from a Humboldt paper:

"Mr. Sunday is a hearty, healthy and happy Christian. He laughs and chats and enjoys the beauties of nature just as any other mortal. He likes to see people happy. He likes to point out to them that there can be no real happiness here or hereafter without doing right. He wins men to the kingdom of God by getting them to see that there can be no safety in any condition where the conduct and life are displeasing to God. When he preaches he preaches with all his might, and he preaches plainly. He calls a spade a spade, and when he denounces sin he does it in italics. His manner is magnetic, and his smile so winsome that the heart of a misanthrope would go out toward him. When he reaches out to shake hands, and gives that firm, hearty grip, it is time to surrender. Talk with him five minutes, and you will feel that he is an old friend. He carries his baseball suit with him, and plays a game now and then to keep his hand in. There is none of the puffed-up Pharisee about him, and that is why he is so well liked by those to whom he preaches."

The following is taken from a Sibley, Iowa, paper:

" The revival meetings which have been held here for three weeks under the direction of W. A. Sunday, closed on Sunday evening with the largest congregation ever assembled under one roof here. To say that Sibley has been stirred to its foundation is putting it mildly. Such a religious awakening has never been known in this section, and its having been attended with so little of the unusual religious excitement augurs well for the probable permanency of its results. There was a good deal of prejudice and criticism at first, but this soon disappeared as the meeting progressed, for no one could listen to Sunday's earnest preaching from night to night and long doubt his sincerity. He preached the truth so forcibly and clearly that it was soon known to be the truth, and produced deep-seated conviction. Every night the seekers were many, and during the meeting over two hundred and fifty made a start."

A paper at Tabor, Iowa, says this and much more of a meeting Sunday held there:

" There is no putting an estimate upon the great good done by the meeting here. While there are a few who do not like Mr. Sunday's outspoken style, no one can deny that he stirred things up in Tabor as it was never done before, and that the community is vastly better for his having been with us."

From Tabor, Sunday went to Tecumseh, Neb., and the local paper there had this to say:

" The union revival meetings under the direction of W. A. Sunday have continued during the past week with constantly growing interest. At night the Presbyterian Church is packed to its utmost capacity. The aisles are filled with chairs, every available foot of space is occupied, and standing room is at a premium. The afternoon meetings are also largely attended, but the great press is at night.

" The church people have already been aroused as never before, and many of them are just beginning to find out what it means to be a Christian. This sounds strange, but it is true. The meetings are also having a very positive and visible effect upon many who have never been affiliated with the church. Mr. Sunday is a plain speaker. He probes under the mask of worldliness and touches many a sore spot that the owner tries to be indifferent about, but Sunday keeps on probing until something has to be done, and that is why some folks do not like him. The truth is a powerful weapon in his hands, and he uses it with great skill."

Of a meeting at Savanna, Ill., the local paper said:

" That much good has resulted is plain to be seen. The churches have been greatly revived. A spirit of unity now exists that was not known before. About two hundred have entered upon a Christian life. Many homes have been gladdened. The ministers can now take up their everyday work, feeling that the cause is dearer than ever, and that their churches are in a much better spiritual condition. The full result of Sunday's labors here has not yet come in. He has done excellent work, and his coming has brought about a state of activity in religious circles that will last. That the people appreciated the meetings was shown by the crowded houses every night."

This is the way he took hold of the little town of Elliott, the scene of one of his earliest meetings in Iowa:

"He is a great power for God, and his preaching is stirring the country for many miles around us. His congregations are sometimes greater than the population of the town. This shows something of what is being done: Wednesday morning the north-bound train brought thirty-five cases of liquor to Elliott, but the south-bound train carried the stuff all back again. Sunday comes out strong against the liquor business, and hits it hard, and hits it where it lives."

A New Hampton, Iowa, paper gave this picture of Sunday in a meeting:

"He does not look like a preacher. He would more likely be taken for a speculator on the stock exchange, or a prematurely old young business man. But when he gets his sails set, and launches out into his sermon, you stop thinking about the man, and have to think of what he is saying, and when he is through you know you have been listening to a genius divinely crowned. Last night he talked for an hour and a half without apparent fatigue, and held the enthralled attention of the vast audience every moment. He may not suit the ultra religionist, but he is getting hold of the people in a wonderful way."

The newspaper reports of a meeting held in southwestern Iowa, at Bedford, the county seat of Taylor

County, fairly show the manner in which a great wave of revival would sweep over a community in a Sunday campaign. Bedford at that time was a typical western town of about two thousand people, and the churches were in anything but a strong spiritual condition. The meetings continued the usual three weeks, during which there were three hundred and eighty-eight conversions, and at the close the free will offering to the evangelist aggregated $968.38, the largest he had ever received. One of the Bedford papers contained this account:

" Never has Bedford witnessed such a religious awakening as is now in progress at the Presbyterian Church. The church of God is being shaken to its very foundation, and many are anxiously inquiring, ' What must I do to be saved?' For nearly a week Evangelist Sunday has been holding great audiences spellbound by the earnest preaching of Christ and him crucified. He has a most forcible manner all his own, that at once commands attention and holds it to the end. He is no more backward in telling church members their shortcomings than he is in commending their virtues. He makes no compromise with the world, the flesh or the devil, and sends plenty of hot shot into the ranks of the sinners. He strikes at everything that bears the stamp of sin with fearlessness and impartiality."

A little later this was said of the meeting:

" Last night ushers brought chairs and filled the aisles, for the people poured in long before the hour of service." And then two or three days further along: " Again the church was crowded to its utmost capacity, not less than thirteen or fourteen hundred being in attendance. Already one hundred and sixty have gone forward and taken a stand for Christ." And still later: " Never in the religious history of this community have there been such meetings as were those of yesterday. The people poured out to the morning meeting and filled the church. In the afternoon the place was packed with men, making the largest audience of men ever assembled in the county at a religious meeting. Some of them drove fifteen miles. Sunday poured hot shot into the sins of the day. As he warmed up off came his collar, then his coat, and for an hour and a quarter he dealt sledge-hammer blows for righteousness. Several times the men burst out in applause that shook the church. They cried and laughed by turns.

"In the evening people began pouring in at five-thirty; women leading children by the hand; young men and maidens, and old men leaning on their canes—everybody. Commodious as the church is, it needed to be as large again to accommodate all who sought seats. The doors were besieged by hundreds, but there was a blockade. The crush was so great that at times there was no moving either backward or forward. Seats were placed in the aisles, and hundreds stood around the walls and by the doors. The platform was thronged.

"The religious interest is becoming deeper every day. People cannot stay away. As a result, the name of God is being revered more than ever before in this community. Never did such crowds assemble to hear the preaching of the gospel. The church is all too small to accommodate the vast throngs that seek admission, and many are the disappointed ones who are turned away. More than two hundred have so far been converted, and still they come. The church is packed long before the time for beginning a meeting, and some people are now driving twenty miles to get here.

"Yesterday was a day of fasting and prayer in Bedford. Cottage prayer meetings are being held in several sections every morning, and a deep religious fervor prevails among the people. The attendance at the church is over thirteen hundred every night, and many are turned away. (Population of town at that time, 2,000.) The afternoon services are largely attended and are having splendid results.

" The capacity of the church was overtaxed again last night. People began pouring in at five-thirty, and at six-thirty standing room was at a premium. Many who came in the afternoon remained to be sure of seats for the night meeting. These union meetings have been a great thing for the churches and for the whole community. It has been shown that great things can be done when people work together. The bringing together of the membership of the different churches in the great gatherings has brought people in touch with each other who have not before labored together in church work, and by so doing has created a bond of sympathy and unity of feeling and purpose which is certain to result in much permanent good.

" All through the meetings there has not been the slightest hitch, but all have pulled together without the least jealousy. We believe it would be to the interest of all the churches to continue to have union meetings occasionally, to keep up the present fine feeling of fraternity.

" Last Sunday night the union revival services closed at the Presbyterian Church. It was the unanimous opinion of all that the last was the best, and that means a good deal. On that night fifty persons went forward and declared themselves for Christ. Among the number were some of our leading business men, county officials and prominent farmers, young and old. Added to those previously converted, it brought the total number up to three hundred and eighty-eight, who to-day are rejoicing in a new life.

"The vast amount of good that has been accomplished in Bedford and surrounding country in the last twenty-three days seems almost incredible. Never before in the history of Taylor county has there been such a revival. Men's hearts were never touched as they have been during the meeting just closed.

"Mr. Sunday came to us a stranger, but has left behind him thousands of warm, admiring friends. He made no charge for his services, but they were appreciated, and the people gave him a free will offering on the last day. He was overcome by the good will and generosity of the people, and could not find words to express his high appreciation.

"We believe the good accomplished has only just begun, and no one can tell where it will ever stop. Like the ripple set in motion by the casting of a pebble into the water, it will go on and on, expanding and enlarging into ever-widening circles of influence for good.

"There was an overflow meeting at the depot, to bid Mr. Sunday and his party farewell and Godspeed. More than two hundred people were there to say a last good-by, and while waiting for the train all joined heartily in singing some of the gospel hymns that had become so familiar and precious to those who attended the services. The spectacle was indeed an inspiring one, and must have cheered those consecrated people, as they set out on their way to other fields of labor. As the train went on its way, handkerchiefs and hats were waved at the little group standing on the rear platform until it was lost to sight.

"Aside from the direct results of the meeting, it is already beginning to bear fruit in ways that will be permanent. Young men are beginning to work for the organization of a Young Men's Christian Association. Young women, too, are asking for special prayer meetings to be held. Old men and middle-aged men are asking what they can do to further the cause of Christ. We believe the good resulting from these meetings will never all be known this side of eternity."

IX

FROM TENT TO TABERNACLE MEETINGS

MR. SUNDAY continued to hold meetings in the smaller towns and villages with constantly increasing interest. Each meeting was a repetition of the stirring scenes of the one before, with something in the way of intensity added. In every place the evangelist and his helpers were more inspired and encouraged by the uniform and increasing results that crowned their efforts. Such marked and constant success could not but have a most invigorating effect upon the faith of Mr. Sunday. His faith had to grow, and it did. It could not have been otherwise. As he found his prayers being answered and his efforts more and more rewarded, the meaning of the promises was revealed to him in a larger and more definite sense, and he found himself taking hold of the Lord for greater things.

This growing confidence in God on the part of the leader was bound to have a direct influence upon the spirit of each meeting, and made more certain the creation of a revival atmosphere—without which there can be no revival, any more than there can be fire without oxygen. Sunday's uniform success also had a most wholesome influence upon every community into which he went, for days, and sometimes weeks, before his arrival. The people expected much because there had been no failure elsewhere.

The evangelist was also steadily learning from ex-

MR. AND MRS. SUNDAY, PAUL, GEO. MARQUIS AND BILLY JR.

periences in each series of meetings how to make more efficient advance preparation, and this is just as necessary in religious movements of magnitude as in great military campaigns. That Sunday is a great general is soon known by all who have anything to do with one of his meetings. Had this not been true of him he could never have become the great evangelist he is to-day, any more than Moses could have led Israel out of Egypt had he not been a great chieftain.

In great meetings such as Sunday holds, nothing can be left to chance. Great plans must be made, and every detail executed with military precision. Without this he would have met his Waterloo long ago. Careful plans are made by the prince of darkness to defeat every one of the meetings, and if Sunday were not a general of a high order, his overthrow would have been rejoiced in by the devil and his black legions long ago.

Sunday has a grasp of details that seldom omits or overlooks any essential thing. He is a veritable Napoleon in holy warfare, and is no more questioned by his lieutenants in anything he decides upon than the " little corporal " would have been questioned by his field marshals. He also has that other great quality the eminent Corsican possessed in such an exalted degree: The ability to quickly inspire and animate with his own undaunted spirit those who work with him. With a word and a look from him, those who have never been known to lift a finger in religious work will take hold and strive like Trojans for the success of the meeting.

Sunday's next step toward the wide sphere of usefulness he at present occupies was the holding of tent meetings in the summer time, and this, he soon discovered, gave his meetings a wider sweep than before. The novelty of the idea at once arrested public attention, and became a great advertisement. His first tent meeting was at Hawkeye, a little town in Iowa. There he not only did the preaching and looked after the choir, but he also had to take care of the tent. Many a night when the wind blew, and the storm beat upon the swaying canvas, Billy would have to jump out of bed and run to sit on the guy ropes, or tighten up a support here and there. The first time he had a singer with him was in 1898, in a meeting he held at Oneida, Ill.

From the beginning of his tent meetings there was always widespread interest, and soon the subject of religion would be the one topic of conversation above all others everywhere—in the shop, the store, on the street and in the home. Wherever the people came together they would at once begin to talk of the meetings. They would tell each other of how fine and grand the music was—above anything they had ever known. And then they would fall to and discuss the preaching just as earnestly, telling what there was about it they liked, and pointing out just as frankly whatever there was about it they didn't like.

Conversions were sometimes brought about by one person repeating to another as much of the sermon as was remembered, and the one who listened would be awakened, and go to praying for deliverance from his sin, and this kind of history is still being repeated, on a constantly increasing scale, wherever the Sunday meetings are held. Every man and woman who attended one of the meetings would at once begin to tell every one they met how different the preaching was from any they had heard before. Not different in doctrine, or in the things preached, but in the way the preaching was done. For example, a couple of farmers would meet at the blacksmith shop, and one would say:

"See here, Jones; there never was any preachin' done jes' like that baseball man does it. I tell you, John, he's got more life in him than any two-year-old colt you ever saw. I would never a-b'lieved it if I hadn't a-seen it, that anybody could ever be so much in airnest at jes' preachin'. He's got a platform to stand on more'n as big as two wagon boxes, an' he kivers every inch of it in every sermon he preaches.

"Why, in the meetin' last Sunday afternoon he got so fired up that he tore off both his coat and vest, jerked off his collar an' kervat, an' then rolled up his sleeves as if he was a-goin' to help thrash.

"My, how he does wake folks up, an' keep 'em on the tenterhooks! Go to sleep? Well, I should say not! Not under the preachin' that's done in that tent. Why, John, he pounds his p'ints clear through you, and makes 'em stick out on the other side.

"I thought I'd been a-hearin' ruther strong preachin' all my life, but I never heard none that took hold of me like hisn does. Why, it goes into you like chiggers, John, an' you can't get away from it. Peeled? What? I wouldn't want Mary Ellen to hear this, but I want to tell you that every time I go to that tent I go out of it feelin' as mean as if I had been a-stealin' sheep; an' I ruther b'lieve my old woman ain't gittin' off any lighter, for all the way home last night she didn't have a word to say, an' you've been married long enough to know, John, that when a woman is keepin' her tongue still it's not because she can't think of anything to say. An' what do you think she said to me this mornin'? Why, that she b'lieved she'd drive old Tom to town this afternoon, an' sell the butter an' go to the day meetin'.

"But I most forgot to tell you about the singin'. It's wonderful, John, an' worth goin' miles an' miles to hear. It does beat all catnip the way a hundred or so notebook singers kin pour out the music. But I must be goin'. I see Jim's got them shoes on my hoss at last. Bring all your folks an' come over to the meetin' to-night, John."

Such scenes as the above were repeated over and over again, and some of them miles and miles from where the meetings were being held, and through them the interest was being continually widened and deepened.

The farmers were busy, of course, but that made no difference to them when the full tide was reached, for they found it easier to go to the meetings then than to stay away. And so it was with merchants, mechanics and business men generally. The interest at the big tent became so great that there was no keeping away, and between meetings large groups of men would be seen at various places on the streets, earnestly talking about all they had seen and heard. And what was true of the men was just as true of the women, only they gathered in each other's homes, or did their talking over back-yard fences.

The holding of tent meetings soon opened the way for Mr. Sunday to go into much larger places than those in which he had been working, and in them he won the same success he had previously had. The larger places having better press facilities, wider and earlier publicity was given to the meetings. The small city papers, being more sensational than the small country weeklies, gave more lurid character to their reports, and made everything sensational that could by stretch of the imagination be made to appear so. Soon they began to make snapshot pictures of Sunday in striking attitudes, with which to embellish their high-colored reports. Through these Sunday's fame began to widen and spread, as if on the wings of the wind, and more frequent and more urgent became the calls for meetings.

Among the tent meetings of which it is possible, at this distant day, to obtain any account, was one held at a town in Iowa, and of this meeting a local paper had this to say:

"Billy Sunday spoke last evening to another audience that taxed the capacity of his big tent. For an hour he held the great congregation almost breathless, save for the liberal applause that greeted some of his most salient and pungent remarks. His text was: 'Where art thou?'

"As a painter of word pictures probably no one ever spoke here before who could equal Sunday. When he told the story of Judas betraying Christ; pictured the three groups in the garden of Gethsemane, and described the terrible mental suffering and anguish of the Saviour, as he prayed and wept apart from his disciples, there were not many who could not in imagination see the whole dreadful scene that was but a prelude to the betrayal, mock conviction and crucifixion.

"In his sermon Sunday told the story of the man who appealed to Christ to cast the devil out of his boy, after some of the disciples had vainly tried to do so. He told of the power it would take to cast the devil out of some of the young bucks of our town. 'And there are lots of them here, too, I am told,' said he; 'with shoes more pointed than their intellects; with more collar than character; with more money than morals, and not much of that. Why, the worldly gang in the churches couldn't deliver a boy from a devil the size of a peanut. There are some church members who are hibernating under their church membership. Some who will wander through the world under the guise of Christians, and

when the end comes they will be buried in the big cemetery, a massive stone raised over their heads, and in
letters cold and gray will be inscribed, " Gone home! "
Yes; gone home—home—home——! ' (pointing sugges-
tively to the ground).

" Sunday then likened some members of some churches
to the rural school committee, who were examining an
applicant for the place of teacher.

" ' In teachin' gogafy,' one of the board asked, ' do
you teach that the world is round or flat? '

" The young man replied that he could teach it either
way, and they could take their choice of how they would
have it. It was all the same to him.

" ' And that is the way some preachers preach. They
will put into their sermons just what their congregations
want, and leave out everything they don't want.'

" It was a great congregation. There were old and
young, rich and poor, sitting side by side. The prosperous business man sat by the side of the day laborer,
and the domestic servant sat beside the woman of wealth
and culture, all social distinctions being for the time forgotten. Religion pure and undefiled is a great leveler.
It was Sunday's farewell sermon, and everybody who
could get into the tent or near it was there to hear it.
He preached a great sermon on the Judgment that was
one of the most searching and impressive he has yet
given. A sermon that cannot soon be forgotten by those
who heard it.

" At the close many responded to his earnest invitation
to make an unconditional surrender of themselves to
Christ. For fifteen minutes men, women and children
thronged the aisles on their way forward. And then at
the close of the meeting hundreds almost fought their
way to the front to shake hands with the noted evan-

gelist, and for thirty minutes laughter from overflowing hearts mingled with tears of joy, as the people still pressed forward to shake the hand of the man who had so stirred our city."

For some time longer Sunday continued to hold tent meetings in the summer, and during the winter in the largest permanent auditoriums available, and with unbroken success wherever he went. All this time he was growing as a preacher, learning both by the large experience in the field, and by burning the midnight oil, for he was a diligent student, and continued to find great ledges of gold in his Bible, the Book which has always been to him beyond all others. As he grew in power, experience and ability, his reputation also grew, spreading from a congressional district, or a few counties, to a considerable section of a state, and then to a whole state, and then to another, and another, until his name began to be familiar over a large part of the middle west. This could have but one effect, and that was to awaken a wider and wider demand for his services.

In every community there are people who are constantly praying for a betterment of religious conditions, and whenever they hear of one whose ministry bears the seal of God, their hearts and their desires turn toward him. They long to have their own hearts quickened and strengthened by his preaching, and their lives made more effective by his instruction, that they may become a channel of blessing to others.

As the pressing demand for his services increased, and calls for meetings multiplied, Sunday began to realize that some way must be discovered that would enable him to preach to the people without having to turn so many away for lack even of standing room, and this often after long drives or long journeys by rail had been made to reach the place of meeting. What to do to remedy this he could not for some time imagine, but at length the idea of a tabernacle suggested itself. The first place in which this idea was put into the concrete was at Perry, Iowa. When it was proposed to the business men and ministers who had given Sunday the call for a meeting, they were in for it at once, and so it was decided to build a tabernacle.

Perry was at that time a town of about three thousand, and all the Protestant churches united in the undertaking. A rough board tabernacle was built that only cost seven hundred dollars, and its seating capacity was not over a thousand. This, like others since, was found too small before the meeting closed. At most of the services every available inch of space was occupied, and people were turned away in large numbers.

The meeting ran three weeks, during which there were three hundred conversions, and every one of the churches was put in fine spiritual condition. On the last Sunday a free will offering of $550 was given to Mr. Sunday.

Existing reports of this pioneer meeting are exceedingly meager, but from a scrapbook fragment of a weekly paper of that time the following account of the last Sunday is taken:

" Sunday was a memorable day in the history of our city. Three large audiences crowded the tabernacle. Mr. Sunday preached three of his most effective sermons, and scores took a stand for Christ.

" The current expenses of the meeting, including the rental of the chairs and piano, light, fuel, care of tabernacle, etc., have been about three hundred and fifty dollars. This was met by the basket collections taken each evening. The cost of the tabernacle was seven hundred dollars, but the lumber in it will pay back no little part

THE DAY BEFORE.

WHAT HAPPENED TO SUNDAY'S LAST TENT ON THE CLOS-
ING DAY AT SALIDA, COL.

of this amount. The total cost of the meeting has been $1,300, but in consideration of the great good accomplished, it has been money well invested. In no other way could so small a sum have done so much for the community.

" Mr. Sunday preached a great sermon in the morning that will not soon be forgotten by the packed audience that heard it. In the afternoon he preached with telling effect to the tabernacle filled with men. The service at night was a most impressive one. The subject was temperance and prohibition, and for an hour and a half the evangelist hurled hot shot into the liquor traffic and its friends.

" At the close of both the afternoon and evening services many went forward as seekers of religion. The farewell sermon was preached on Monday evening, and the audience tested the capacity of the house. Again there were many seekers.

" The interest manifested in the Sunday revival meetings was without a parallel in local religious history, and increased rather than diminished up to the time the train left the depot with the noted evangelist on board. From the first sermon it was evident that Mr. Sunday was a man of great natural ability and liberal culture, a fine orator, with an extensive vocabulary, intensely in earnest, and before the end of the first week all knew that he was an expert in evangelistic work. Whatever there may have been in the way of criticism only helped his popularity, and made greater demand for seats in the tabernacle. He was master of the situation, and soon everybody knew it.

" ' What crowds!' was the expression heard every night, and it mattered little what the weather was. When the people once began going nothing could stop them.

" The sermons were all good, without a single exception. Full of sentiment, pathos, argument, good logic, word pictures, impersonation, etc., all used to illustrate and drive home gospel truths. In his arraignment of card playing, dancing and the saloon, he was very much in earnest and remarkably forcible. In fact he was so scathing in his denunciation that some criticised his language, but little he cared. Usually at revivals most of the converts are women and children, but that was not the case here. In fact, just the opposite was true. It is most wonderful the way Sunday gets hold of men, and men of all kinds, but especially so of young men."

Sunday's last tent meeting was held at Salida, Colo., beginning about the fifteenth of September. He had gone there with the assurance that they never had snow at that time of year, and so felt safe on that score. He had the usual results, of a great meeting with deep interest, large attendance, many conversions, and the people urging him to stay longer.

But after the meeting closed on the last Saturday night, storm clouds filled the heavens, and a little later filled the air with frost and snow. The next morning when Sunday opened his eyes from the peaceful slumber in which the night had wrapped him, and looked out upon the new day, he was horrified to find snow to the right of him, snow to the left of him, snow in front of him, and snow something like three or four feet deep everywhere. The tent was loaded down and crushed with it, and the streets were impassable. It was all the more disheartening because that was the closing day of the meeting, and the time when the people were to show how much they appreciated his strenuous labors among them by giving him a free will offering.

However, such a revival as had come from Sunday's

intensely practical preaching could not but bring to the surface a few good Samaritans who soon found their way to him and began to cheer his heart with the golden speech that "doeth good like a medicine." And then soon others like them began to go out "into the streets and lanes of the city," with improvised snow-plows, and by church time it was made possible for those in every part of the village to reach the place of worship.

Many willing hands had done what they could toward putting the tent in condition for the services, but this was soon found to be out of the question, and arrangements had to be made for taking the meeting into the public hall, which in a small village is always dignified with the name of "Opera House," but it could not accommodate half the people the tent would have held. But the people had a mind to give, and Sunday did not have to walk home, though it is doubtful if he ever had a greater scare.

X

STYLE AND CHARACTER OF SUNDAY'S PREACHING

MUCH preaching is done over the heads of the people, but this is never true of Sunday. He gets down to where the people live, and talks so plainly that they know what he means. He has the gift of tongues, but his speech is never Greek to any one. Little children are as much interested as the grown-ups, for they know what he means about as well as college professors. He could, no doubt, sandpaper and polish his sermons until they would be admired as works of art, but that is all they would be, and the market is overstocked with that kind now. And then Sunday does not preach for admiration, or he would cut his stick differently. Some preachers do, but not Billy Sunday. What he wants is results that will stand the fires of the Judgment, and that is why in every sermon he tries to land under the fifth rib. He can be eloquent, and often is; wondrously so, but that is incidental, and not the thing for which he preaches.

One of the most notable characteristics of Sunday's preaching is that it is always interesting. No matter what he talks about he has undivided attention, and holds it without effort as long as he cares to talk. He is interesting because he is so picturesque. He makes you see things, and see them in an interesting way. Darwin wrote a book on angleworms that reads like a romance.

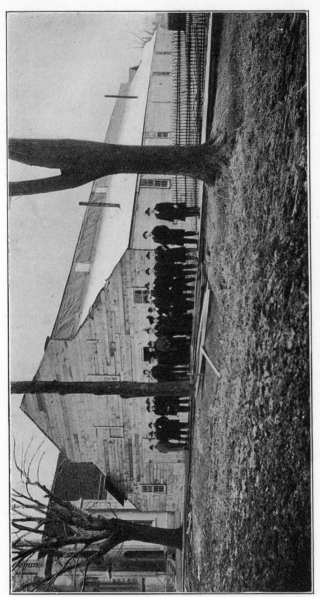

ONE OF THE EARLIER TABERNACLES.

Sunday could talk about a rail fence and make you see more beauty in its vineclad nooks and corners than another could show you in a cathedral. He has an imagination that can make the most commonplace things as radiant with beauty as fairyland. He can paint pictures with words, and pictures, too, that you can see as plainly as any an artist ever painted with colors. Sunday is interesting, not because he describes things, but because he holds them up before you and makes you see them as you never did before.

Sunday is interesting because he uses plain and simple language when he preaches, and you don't have to have an open dictionary in your lap to make out what he means. He throws no Latin or Greek at your head, and takes up no time in telling what this clause or that means in the original. He uses the plainest kind of English, and the most expressive he can find. He calls things by their right names, even if to do so he has to use words that almost burn and blister. It is doubtful if any living preacher can pour out such a stream of red-hot and sizzling adjectives to show the scorn and withering contempt he feels for all that bears the name of sin as Billy Sunday. When he stands in the pulpit with his open Bible before him, he fears neither man nor devil, and in the terrific and almost tragic manner in which he thunders against whatever he believes to be wicked, you can almost see the lightning flashes of Sinai. There are moments when he makes you think of the way in which the Master denounced the scribes, Pharisees and hypocrites in the twenty-third chapter of Matthew. With no more fear than Elijah had when he stood before Ahab, he tears the mask from sin, and makes it stand before you a false and cruel thing that is devilish and wicked.

While he thunders terrific denunciations against the

sins that people right there before him are guilty of, without thought or care as to where his burning shafts will strike, blanched faces may be seen all over the tabernacle. And whatever he says he says standing on the Rock of Ages, with a " thus saith the Lord " for the stand he takes, so that you are compelled to see that God is against the thing he denounces, as plainly as Belshazzar saw the handwriting on the wall. By his remarkable gift of utterance, expression and illustration he shows how relentlessly and persistently the devil, working through the allurements of fashionable society, finds a way to run his claws into our boys, girls and young people and drag them headlong to perdition.

Portraying most vividly, by word and action, the character of the sin he denounces, he shoots into the audience volley after volley of gospel hot shot, until many before him pale and tremble with conviction. Sunday has thorough conversions because he preaches in a way that produces deep conviction. People strain to catch every word he utters, for they are full of expectancy, knowing that he has the courage to lay bare popular sins to the teeth, and show how churches, homes and society are rank with hypocrites, cowards and big sinners, and when he has finished the worst man has to admit to his own soul that for once he has heard the Bible truth. But after telling the multitudes of their individual sinfulness, as no other man can do it, he points the way of deliverance so plainly and convincingly that scores and hundreds at a time crowd forward to accept the great gift that God has offered to all repentant.

Does Sunday use slang? Well, yes—some; but what is slang but language in the making, and unconventional speech? Carefully study the Bible characters whom God has used, and how many will you find of the stereotyped kind? In what respect was Moses like other men? Was it not a band of ram's horns that led Joshua's army to victory? How much of a part did the silver trumpets have in that campaign? Didn't Samson thin the ranks of the enemy with the jawbone of an ass? Didn't David use a sling, and Shamgar an oxgoad? And then there was Gideon's band, with their lamps, pitchers and trumpets, and remember that the Master himself "taught not as the scribes." These were all unconventional methods, but notice that they brought more than conventional results. When some evangelist who never uses slang begins to shake the world for God in a way more glorious than Sunday has done, it will be time enough to condemn its use as an unpardonable sin. No man has ever been much of a leader unless he had the courage to step off alone.

Jesus did not preach and teach in classical Greek, but in the common everyday speech of the common people; the language of the street and the market place.

In a place where Sunday was to hold a meeting, a delegation of ministers requested him to "smooth down" his preaching. He smiled, and said:

"Why, if I did that I wouldn't have any more people to preach to than you men do."

Does he use illlustrations? Plenty of them, and good ones, too. He couldn't preach without them, and after hearing him once you would never want him to. Too many long sermons are iike a blank wall, without a picture or a window anywhere. Whoever hears any of Sunday's preaching will be able to carry away enough of it to awaken somebody. His illustrations always illustrate, and make you see things.

The gospel Sunday preaches is the same as Jesus and his disciples preached. The same as the apostles wrote

of in their epistles. It fits the millionaire as well as
does the man who toils for his bread. To listen
Sunday is to find yourself with a blown-out tire, if y(
are a hypocrite. If you are not right with God you w
know it before he has been preaching ten minutes. Y(
will begin to hate your life and your sins the insta
you get a glimpse of the Christ he preaches. You w
see that all sin is from the devil, and must be punish
and banished somewhere.

One of Sunday's greatest meetings was held
Wilkes-Barre, Pa., and a correspondent of the *Record*
that city, who closely studied him while there, had tl
to say:

" He has skimmed the literature of the English race f
information and illustrations, and has a slang vocabula
that is simply astounding. He uses his knowledge wi
such telling effect that ' those who come to scoff rema
to pray.' His earnestness, his transparent honesty, c;
ries his hearers with him, and his slang is all forgott
in his clarion call for repentance; his denunciation
all that is bad, vile and wicked, and in his praise of G(
home and country.

" The old school of evangelists were of the itinera
class, moving rapidly through the country, their evang
ism seemed sudden in its effects, and I am afraid son
what evanescent in its results. It is just here that St
day's campaign gives promise of more lasting good. I
coming has been carefully prepared for, and his meeti
place is undenominational and unconventional in ch;
acter. His is a movement conducted with great busin(
acumen and sound common-sense. He trains the m
isters and church workers in such a way as to ma
them capable of caring for the harvest when it com
Like a good farmer, he prunes the fruit trees with vig(

cuts out all the dead wood and sprays well to get rid of moths, beetles and ' such like,' so that when the new fruit shall ripen it will be sound and good. Mr. Sunday is a man with a great faith. He prays for the blessing, he prepares for the blessing, and he is sure of getting it. It is theretore no surprise to him when it comes.

" The late revival in Wales was a marvelous spontaneous outburst of religious fervor, and roused large sections of country. It was conducted by a young man named Roberts, who being ill-fitted, both mentally and physically, subsequently broke down, just when a leader was most needed. Want of well-directed effort, want of unity on the part of the churches in looking after and caring for the converts robbed the movement of much of its success. The Sunday campaign is conducted vastly different. It is an old evangel, presented in racy, striking and modernized speech, and conducted on up-to-date business principles. The churches are a unit, and the movement has been aided by the newspapers in obtaining a publicity unknown to the fathers. Despite a few doubting Thomases the spirit of success is in the air; a great and glorious revival is upon us, the effects of which are sure to continue."

Travelers in the desert have often described the palm tree to us. Telling of its loveliness and beauty of form, usefulness, etc., but no matter how graphically they picture it, we must see the tree for ourselves before we can know what they mean, and the case is just as true of Mr. Sunday. Little can be known of him until he has been seen and heard. We can read all the newspapers have to say about him, and hear all that those who have seen him may be able to tell us, and yet have an altogether wrong opinion of the man. We mav read his printed sermons, and hear others recite all they can remember of them. We may be told of what he says and how he says it, by those who claim to know him, and yet be at sea as to his real personality until we have seen and heard him for ourselves.

While he was holding a meeting at South Bend some time ago, Rev. T. J. Giblett, pastor of the First Baptist Church, Mishawaka, had this to say of him:

"The one question upon the lips of every one is, 'Have you heard Billy Sunday yet?' and if the answer is in the affirmative the next question is, 'Well, what do you think of him?' Varied are the replies, but most of them can be summed up in a sentence or two which runs somewhat like this: 'Great!' or 'Wonderful!' or 'He's all right!' The knocker has turned booster, the skeptic has become convinced, the admiration of the friend and well-wisher has deepened into love and championship.

"No one can doubt the absolute sincerity of the man. The downright earnestness which literally consumes his being. He is a Daniel come to judgment, a Savonarola denouncing the sins of the people, an Isaiah pointing to God as the solution of great public questions. A Jeremiah burdened on account of the sins and sorrows of the people, and beseeching them to turn to the Lord for salvation. The common people hear him gladly because he understands their life. The well-to-do and cultured flock to his meetings, listen to his burning words, his fierce denunciation of their sins and weaknesses; yet return again and again for more, and are numbered among his staunchest friends.

"You cannot explain his marvelous success on any other basis than that God is with him. His closest associates have said that he is a man of God, and his whole

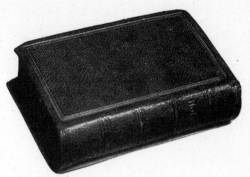

MY FIRST BIBLE.

I bought this at a second-hand store in St. Louis, in 1886,
for 35 cents. I wouldn't take $3,500 for it to-day.

W. A. Sunday.
v. Tim. 2: 15.

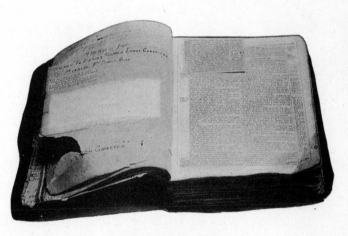

A WORN-OUT BIBLE.

attitude attests the truth of the statement. I have no criticism to offer as to the work done in South Bend. If any prejudice ever lurked in my mind it has been dispelled and expelled since the campaign began. His language is not always as dignified and precise as that of the average pulpit to-day, but if he talked as we ministers usually do, he would have no more success in getting the crowd than we do. And there is something very refreshing in having things called by their right names, as also is the absence of wriggling diplomacy to avoid saying things that cut.

" Nathan the prophet, who said to David, ' Thou art the man ! ' seems to be reincarnate in Billy Sunday, and the average man who listens to him evidently enjoys that kind of preaching. I am looking for a mighty army to come out on the side of the Lord in South Bend. The work among the men is going to be the most telling feature in the campaign. Sunday after Sunday ten thousand men listen attentively and enthusiastically to a magnificent appeal for a clean life, and this must surely have a most beneficial effect upon the whole community."

During the South Bend meeting, J. Andrew Boyd, managing editor of the Wilkes-Barre *Record,* wrote as follows to the *Tribune* of that city :

" Of course there are some church members who will not go to hear Sunday. They may be looked up to and respected by the community, but if they are, it is because the community does not know them. They are living a dual life, and they do not want the sword of the Spirit, as it is wielded by Billy to lay bare the rottenness of their lives. They don't want to have their consciences disturbed. They have been crying, ' Peace, peace,' so long that they don't want to be told that ' there is no peace, saith my God, for the wicked.' They don't like to smell brimstone. They want deodorized and disinfected sermons of tabloid size. Sermons about the birds that sing in the wood, the flowers that bloom in the spring, and babbling brooks that sing on their way to the sea, rather than sermons about the song of the redeemed and the Rose of Sharon, and the Water of Life.

" Then there are the women of culture, and the women of society, who will not go to hear Billy. Why? Because with their pink teas, their bridge and theater parties, and the care of their poodles, they have no time. Why should they cut out pink teas and such fol-de-rols, to sit on a wooden bench, with their feet on a sawdust floor, to hear a man ' reason of righteousness, temperance and judgment to come '? Why should they give up bridge, when there are still pieces of cut glass and chocolate pots and bric-a-brac to be had for the shuffling of the pasteboards? Of course they won't go to hear him. They think too much of their precious skins, and don't want to be flayed alive, or shown up as the whitened sepulchres that they are.

" It needs no prophet to say that the booze slingers will not go to hear Billy. They have no use for him in their business, and their business and Billy's business won't mix any more than oil and water will mix. Besides, they have tender hides, and don't care to have them peppered as full of holes as a screen door. The whisky man knows that he will get his good and proper if he goes to hear Billy. The brewer's big horses can't run over Sunday. He is no more afraid of them than a child is of a kitten. No man of modern times has given the saloon such a scare and such a lambasting as it gets from Billy Sunday, and ' there's a reason ' why they don't like him.

" Of course there are a few others who will not go

to hear him, but generally speaking, there are not many outside the classes mentioned above. But none of these will be missed from the crowds that will hear him, and for every one opposed to him there are hundreds who favor him, and believe in him, and before he closes his campaign in South Bend, his traducers and vilifiers will be hunting holes to crawl into—and a mighty small hole will answer for the biggest of them."

XI

LAST DAY OF THE BURLINGTON MEETING

SUNDAY'S meeting at Burlington, Iowa, was one of his greatest up to that time, and attracted wide attention. This chapter is taken from the *Hawkeye's* report of the closing day, and was written by Dr. G. Walter Barr, a journalist of Keokuk:

"Rev. W. A. Sunday's labors of five weeks closed in Burlington amid a scene of wild enthusiasm. A half acre of fluttering handkerchiefs and cheers from six thousand throats, shouting in a delirium of feeling, after twenty-five hundred persons had been added to the membership of Burlington churches, with hundreds more giving notice of their coming a little later. After this staid old city, firm in the conservatism of a one-time capital of Iowa, had been faced about and given such an uplift of moral standard that the observer within its gates who saw its intense antagonism six weeks ago, is overwhelmed with amazement at the change.

"After this man showed oratorical ability strong enough to pack a huge structure, with four to six thousand people at every session, and to have the largest attendance at the end of five weeks constant speaking. After the topmost item in the data of the table of history of revivalism in America had been surpassed, and the wonderful work of Australia, Wales and England had been equaled. After local ministers assisting him had collapsed and gone to bed broken down, and wiry

116

newspaper men accustomed to the strenuous life were on the verge of exhaustion, this most remarkable man in the world to-day ended a day of three tremendous sermons, as chipper as a newly elected candidate, and in a voice still able to carry half a mile, shouted:

" 'Farewell, fellow sinners; I'm free from your blood!'

" The last scene of the drama so full of the strongest heart throbs of humanity as to be a tragedy many times; so full of the unusual climacteric as to be thrilling at times; with something of comedy at times; the last scene may indicate something of the tremendousness of what has occurred here in the last five weeks.

" It is half past seven o'clock of a Sabbath evening in the tabernacle on West Hill. The building of thin pine boards and long roof trusses is packed with a solid mass of people so tightly that women faint in the crush, and strong men find their arms pinioned to their sides. Full six thousand people are in that mass of humanity that is quiet, because it has no chance to move. They all sing gospel songs in a grand chorus, such as was never heard in Iowa before. Then a man with a pleasant face and an iron-gray imperial advances a step nearer to the high pulpit edge of the platform, at one end of the crowded building, and says a few words of appreciation of this evangelist and his work.

" The waves that have been toppling the great tidal swell for weeks break over in whitecaps. The level plain of a half-acre of heads becomes a lake of white hand-kerchiefs wildly waving at arm's length. Cheer after cheer goes up, reminding one of the roar of national conventions when presidents are made. Time after time the waves of feeling break into whitecaps, and the cheers resound to the rafters and the sky. That was Burlington's answer to the request that all who have learned to love and respect William A. Sunday should indicate their feeling toward him.

" The background of this picture was the surging measure of song that rolled out in the big tabernacle from thousands of voices, led by the chorus choir of hundreds, as the people sung what was in their hearts. After the final evening sermon, and long after the preacher of it had gone to his rest, the people remained and sang.

" ' When the roll is called up yonder, I'll be there! ' had new meaning to some of them.

" ' The Sweet By-and-By ' was nearer than ever to some of them.

" ' Shall we gather at the river? ' was answered by an increased volume of sound at the verse—

" ' Yes, we'll gather at the river! '

" ' Blest be the tie that binds,' was chanted over and over again between other hymns, as ' My Jesus, I love thee,' and ' Where He leads I'll follow,' for ' I surrender all,' this last song of the famous ' Little Red Book,' was sung over and over again, and then repeated at the end once more.

" These things were the end of a day of almost continual procession of great things occurring in a moving panorama. The greatest scene of the day was the men's meeting in the afternoon, when between four and five thousand stood to pledge their practical support at the polls and elsewhere, to the mayor, if he shall close the saloons on Sunday, and exterminate the gambling houses in Burlington.

" They did it with cheers and apparent determination. That was a climax harmonizing with the sermon to the effect of the liquor traffic on human society, which was full of figures and facts. It was a sermon of such strenuosity that soon after the text this battleship of a man was firing his thirteen-inch battery, stripped for action, without coat, cuffs, collar or vest.

" The morning sermon was a sort of musical symphony of oratory, with constantly recurring motif: ' Look to yourselves, that ye receive a full reward ! '

" The evening sermon had another of those refrains which are so common in the pulpit product of this remarkable preacher, that roar out at times, and again ring like a trumpet, and then come back time and again softly, like echoes from the bluffs, to be sent out again in a shout, and come again in an echo. The refrain of the evening sermon was the one word:

" ' To-morrow ! ' and its harmonic was:

" ' E-t-e-r-n-i-t-y ! '

" The sermon was the strongest possible expression of the human soul struggling in the greatest possible feeling of responsibility, and it lifted some of the responsibility from the shoulders of the preacher to the hearts of his auditors. It was a story rich in those flowering stories each of which has a fruition of a lesson at the end.

" ' The peroration of the entire series of meetings included a little poem, which this excellent elocutionist read in a most impressive way. It had for its keynote—

" ' We scarce know our friends,
        Till we have bid them farewell.'

" Rev. William A. Sunday made it express something of his own feelings, as he bade farewell to Burlington, and it was appropriate, for it was full of religious fervor.

" The coming of the three hundred and forty converts of the last day was a scene worthy of better description than it ever will have. The center of the cyclone was at the end of the afternoon sermon, when strong men pushed their way through the crowded building to reach the helping hand extended to them from the edge of the purple platform above their heads. In a minute after the invitation was given the aisles were jammed like the Chippewa river is sometimes with pine logs. Then the jam broke loose, and the current of men rushed down and into the seats which the ushers were rapidly clearing in front.

" Workers were running around, and stirring up the mass of people which had packed the tabernacle until the very walls were strained. Others were trying to make paths for the seekers to travel to the cleared space in front of the platform, upon which stood this man Sunday, who had stirred up the seething, boiling, churning maelstrom of humanity to make a picture not often seen in the whole world.

" Sometimes he stood leaning over the edge of the high platform, reaching down his hand to the men stretching up their hands from below, with gestures like that of a man in paintings, reaching from the edge of the ship's rescuing boat.

" ' Come on, men ! ' was the cry constantly resounding from the leader in action, as desperately vital and strong as ever was seen in a commander leading a charge in the crisis of a battle ; and men rallied to his colors.

" The call for converts at the other two services of the Sabbath was less loud, but equally determined. In the morning there was immediate response to the invitation, and a steady stream came down the aisles for a short time without any urging, until fifty men had responded.

" The evening call for converts was less urgent, but very intense in its earnestness. The building was so densely packed at the last meeting that they had fairly to fight their way down the aisles which checked the stream at first, but in five minutes the way had been cleared, so that they came down in a steady current, faster and faster, until one hundred and fifty-one persons occupied the front seats.

"Most of the audience—enough to make the tabernacle seem filled—stood up to watch the moving picture at the front, most of them standing on the benches. Frequently applause broke out, as some prominent man reached up his hand to the platform, and turned to the seats provided for the seekers.

"Perhaps the loudest applause was when there came down a side aisle, and across the space in front of the platform, a man with a mass of silver-gray hair, topping a very strong face, a high forehead and a large head with many cranial curves suggestive of Robert E. Lee—a man whose head and features would attract attention anywhere, and who seemed to be specially the object of regard here in Burlington, where he has been a school principal for many years."

XII

EXTRACTS FROM SERMONS

SOMETIMES the unpardonable sin may be utter and absolute indifference. Some can hear any sermon and any song, and still remain unmoved. I'll venture that some of you have not been convicted of sin for twenty-five years. No matter what you do, your conscience never hurts you. Back yonder somewhere the Spirit of God convicted you, but you didn't yield. The first place I ever preached, in my own meeting, was in the little town of Garner, Hancock County, Iowa. As a man came down the aisle I said, " Who is that?" and some one told me it was one of the richest men in the county. I asked him what I had said to help him, and he replied, " Nothing."

Then he told me that twenty-one years before he had gone to Chicago and sold his stock, four hours before he had to catch a train. Moody was in town holding a meeting, and with a friend the Garner man had gone and stood inside the door, listening to the sermon. When Moody gave the invitation he handed his coat and hat to his friend, and said he was going forward. The friend told him not to do it, or he would miss his train, and that his railroad pass would be no good after that day. He said he could afford to pay his way home. His friend told him not to go up there amid all the excitement, but to wait and settle it at home. He said he had waited thirty-five years without settling it at home, but his friend finally prevailed, and they left to make the train, without first going forward, as he had so much desired to do.

He told me that he had never afterward had the slightest desire to be a Christian, in all that twenty-one years, until he heard me preach that night. Had he been deaf to that call I doubt if he would ever have had another.

———

I don't care if a church has two thousand members. What I ask is, how much power have they? Nine times out of ten you blame the evangelist when there are no conversions, instead of the God-forsaken, booze-hitting card-playing church members. There were places where Jesus could do no mighty works because of unbelief where there should have been faith. As unbelief increases faith decreases, and that's the trouble with too many churches to-day. What the church needs isn't pipe organs. They're all right, but they won't bring power. You can never move any mountains with them. I think God ought to have the finest buildings and the finest decorations. I believe in them. Nothing can ever be too fine for him, but faith is the only thing that can ever roll the mountains into the sea.

Faith is to us what a trolley is to a street car. The trolley is the means by which the power gets from the dynamo to the motor, and the motor is what makes the car go. I cannot touch God with my hands, but I can touch you. You are material; God is spiritual. Faith is the hand of the soul, and it is with it we must touch God. There is a law of faith as positive as the law of electricity. We get results from electricity, when we obey its law, whether we understand it or not. We do as electricity commands, and it gives us power without

stint. When we obey God's spiritual laws just as fully
—and by these I mean the laws of faith—he will take up
our mountains and throw them into the sea for us.
When we obey the law of electricity we have physical
power, and when we obey the law of faith we have
spiritual power. That's all there is to it. One is as
certain as the other, for the same God is back of both.
It is the most common-sense thing in the world, this
religion. You say you don't understand it. You don't
have to understand electricity to ride on a street car, do
you? You don't have to understand it to send a tele-
graph message, or talk over the telephone. So do what
God tells you in religion, whether you understand it or
not, and you will get results that will convince and satisfy
you. "If any man will do his will he shall *know*."
There will be no guesswork about it. The trouble with
too many churches is, that while they have fine church
buildings, fine organs, fine pews, fine music and fine
preaching, they are not in connection with the power
house. You don't have to break the wheels and smash
in the sides of a traction car to make it stand still. Just
break the connection and the light goes out, and there
you are.—*Sermon on Faith*.

A man says, " I do not believe the Bible because there
are inconsistencies in it." I say, the greatest inconsistency is not in the Bible, but in your life. I bring to
that man the memory of an awful deed, and he immediately begins to find fault with the Bible. You talk
business or politics with him, and he will talk sense.
Talk religion, and he will talk nonsense.

I said to a barkeeper one time, " Why don't you give
your heart to Christ? You are too nice a fellow to be

in this vile business." He said, "I wouldn't be in it
if the church members hadn't voted for me."

If there is anything that makes me sick, it is to have
some red-nosed, buttermilk-eyed, beetle-browed, peanut-
brained, stall-fed old saloon keeper say that he wouldn't
be in the business if it were not for the church members
voting for him. Hell is so full of such church members
that their feet are sticking out of the windows.

Dr. Arnold, of Rugby, once wrote a letter to Dean
Swift, in which he said: " Whenever a day comes when
I can receive a boy into my school without emotion, it
will be time for me to be off." Whenever a day comes
when I can stand and preach God's word without an
agony of anxiety lest the people will not accept Christ;
whenever a day comes when I can see men and women
coming down the aisles without joy in my heart, I'll quit
preaching.

The proof of the pudding is not in smelling the bag
or chewing the string, but in eating it, and yet there are
lots of men who try to decide the value of Christianity
by smelling the bag and chewing the rag over some
hypocrites in the church. That is an easy matter, for it
requires no brains, or sense, or thought; very little reading, and less yet of observation.

I was in Washington not long ago, and went into the
Secret Service Department, and there my friend, Chief
Wilkie, took me to the room where they keep the money
made by counterfeiters, and the tools with which they
make it. Now, when I saw that stuff, that money that
was no good, do you think I went down into my pocket

and took out the good silver dollar I had there and threw it away, just because I saw all that bad money? Not much I didn't. My one good dollar would buy more than all that counterfeit stuff. That is just what a lot of you fellows are doing who are not Christians. because there are hypocrites in the church.

I have been told that a dove has been known to tremble when a single feather from a vulture's wing has been held in front of it. I do not know whether this is a fact, but I do know that the Holy Spirit trembles and is grieved by the actions and indifference of some of you church members. I know it because I know that God loves us, and where there is love there will be grief at wrong-doing.

Everybody knows that in this day and age the farmer who would do his plowing with a crooked stick would be set down as a fool. The farmer who has sense uses the best plow and farm machinery he can get, and would not for a minute think of farming as his great grand-father did. Bishop Taylor promised God he would do as much hard thinking and planning for him as he would do for any man for money, and he did it. So did John Wesley and Whitefield and Savonarola, and look what they did for God! If there is any better way of doing God's work to-day than there was a hundred years ago, in heaven's name let us do it in that way. He is entitled to the very best possible.

This thing of just ringing the church bell to get people to attend is bigger fool business than it would be for the farmer of to-day to plow with a crooked stick. Things are not run that way in the business world. In business the machine or method that is out of date goes to the scrap heap, but in religion we hold on to it until it is covered with moss a foot thick, and say with a pious whine, " Surely it is not God's set time to work! " In business a better machine and a better method always drives out a poorer one, but in religion we are hundreds of years behind the time, and then we blame God because we are boneheads. In religion we do our fighting with the same old smoothbore flintlock muskets, and climb up Zion's hill in the same old stage coaches, over corduroy roads, and if anybody hints at a better way we roll our eyes and look as if we had on a hair shirt, as again we say, " Surely this is not God's set time to work! "

I tell you any time is God's time. Now is God's time. It was God's time to give us electricity long before Franklin discovered it, but everybody was too thick-skulled to know it. It was God's time to give us the electric light long before Edison invented it, but nobody had sense enough to understand it. It was God's time to give us the steam engine long before Watt watched the teakettle boil, and saw it puff the lid off, but nobody had sense enough to grasp the idea. Had we been as boneheaded in invention and business as we have been in religion, we would hardly be out of the stone age yet. Give yourself to God outright, and be willing to wake up and climb up, and you'll soon find yourself doing lots of things that will astonish you and the old crowd you have been so long buried with. No man can ever know the amazing power that lies dormant in him, until God gets complete control of his individuality.

D. L. Moody was a shoe salesman, and never discovered the power that was in him until God got hold of him and set him to work. Jerry McAuley was an old wharf rat until he gave himself as a living sacrifice

to God. Andrew, the humble disciple, was an obscure
and lowly man until God took him in hand. We make
our store windows blaze with electric light, and keep
them that way, even on dark days, and yet allow so many
of our churches to look like a London fog on prayer
meeting night. If a man has joy and love and peace
inside, he dishonors God if he goes around looking as
if he had no friends on earth or in heaven. Give your
face to God and He will put His shine on it. If you
are one of the long-faced brand of Christians, get rid
of it. God never put such a face on you. That's the
kind of faces the Pharisees had, and Jesus said their
faces were disfigured. When a man tries to make himself, without asking God to help him, he is sure to have
a face as long as a smokestack—more or less. I tell you
the devil will bank his fire and go to church to hear a
man like that give testimony. God doesn't want you to
look and act as if your religion affected you like the
toothache. If it does it isn't God's kind.—*Sermon on
Consecration.*

———

At one place where I was holding a meeting in Iowa,
a young man went out, and he was mad. He went out
storming and raving, cussing and damning the preacher
and the church, and everything and everybody; declaring
that he didn't believe in God; didn't believe in Jesus
Christ; didn't believe in inspiration; didn't believe the
Bible; didn't believe in anything.

That fellow was a Knight Templar, and the next evening, I was told, the lodge had an all-night session with
the young man, trying to make him see the error of his
ways. I said to the friend who told me this:

"Did you throw him out of the lodge?"

"BILLY" JR.

" Oh, no," he said.

" Why didn't you?" I asked. " Your lodge believes in God and in the Bible, and this fellow don't. Why don't you put him out?"

And yet they complain about the hypocrites in the churches. They've got plenty of them in every lodge. Is that an argument against the lodge? Of course not, unless you are an unadulterated fool. There isn't a church in this city that hasn't got a lot of hypocrites in it. Is that an argument against the churches? Certainly not.

―――

Where you put salt it kills the bacteria that cause decay. If a man were to take a piece of meat and smell it and look disgusted, and his little boy were to say:

" What's the matter with it, pop?" and he should say:

" It is undergoing a process in the formation of new chemical compounds," the boy would be all in; he wouldn't understand. But if his father were to say:

" It's rotten!" then the boy would understand and hold his nose. Perhaps this will be all some of you need to know why I preach as I do.

" Rotten " is a good Anglo-Saxon word, and you don't have to go to the dictionary to know what it means. Some of you preachers better look out, or the devil will get away with some of your members before they can find out what you mean in your sermons.

You notice I use a good many Anglo-Saxon words, and I do it not only to save time, but to save some of the people who don't have a whole bookcase in their heads.

" A process in the formation of new chemical compounds," is just the Bostonese way of saying a thing is rotten. It's the society way of trying to keep from holding your nose, because it's vulgar, but I like " rotten " because it gets over the line quicker. Too many preachers are doing all their preaching according to the Bostonese, but I believe in ringing the fire bell before the house burns down.

———

Every nation must have its vision of God, or go down. Where now is Babylon? Gone! Where now is Rome? Gone! and all we know about it comes from " Gibbon's Rise and Fall of the Roman Empire." Where now is Greece? Gone! and Straubau tells us about its glory.

If America has the sins of Babylon she will have the punishment of Babylon, and don't you think she won't. Don't think that because you can stand around and boast of her glories, and say you can build a wall around her and live on what is produced inside, without the aid of any outside nation, and boast of her wealth and her power, that she will not be punished for sin. These things are all right. You have the right to tell of them, but let us remember there is another side. If we put God out, all of the wealth and all of the power on earth will not stay the judgment.

———

Out in Boulder, Colo., I attended a miners' picnic, a great affair that is held each year, and I saw a drilling contest there. Two men would take a drill and bore a hole in a block of solid granite, and they would keep a hose turned on the drill to prevent it from becoming too hot.

There isn't much that is interesting in drilling a hole

in a block of granite, is there? Yet that crowd applauded, and pretty soon I found myself standing up, so that I could see better, and I found myself applauding, too. I was wonderfully interested in that contest. Two men bored a hole twenty-eight inches deep in ten minutes. If two men drilling a hole in a block of granite can create more interest, and hold the attention of a great crowd more than I can in preaching Christ and Him crucified, I'll know it's time for me to be off.

———

Don't be afraid to use your light. Don't turn it down as you do the gas to keep the meter from running so fast. I hate to visit in the home in which there is a fussy woman following you around, turning down the gas. Let your light burn full and bright so that everybody can see it, and be made happier by it. You ought to live so that every one who comes near you will know that you are a Christian? Do you? Does your milkman know that you are a Christian? Does the man who brings your laundry know that you belong to church? Does the man who hauls away your ashes know that you are a Christian? Does your newsboy know that you have religion? Does the butcher know that you are on your way to heaven? Some of you buy meat on Saturday night, and have him deliver it Sunday morning, just to save a little ice, and then you wonder why he doesn't go to church.

If you had to get into heaven on the testimony of your washerwoman, could you make it? If your getting into heaven depended on what your dressmaker knows about your religion, would you land? If your husband had to gain admittance to heaven on the testimony of his stenographer, could he do it? If his salvation depended on what his clerks tell about him, would he get there? A man ought to be as religious in business as he is in church. He ought to be as religious in buying and selling as he is in praying.

There are so many church members who are not even known in their own neighborhood as Christians. Out in Iowa where a meeting was being held, a man made up his mind that he would try to get an old sinner into the kingdom, and after chasing him around for three days he finally cornered him. Then he talked to that old fellow for two hours, and then the old scoundrel stroked his whiskers, and what do you think he said? " Why, I've been a member of the church down there for fourteen years." Just think of it! A member of the church for fourteen years, and a man had to chase him three days, and talk with him for two hours to find it out.—*Sermon on " Let your light shine."*

Billy Sunday's sermons are like life itself. Tears and smiles and sighs and laughter; the solemn and the absurd, the commonplace and the exalted are mingled together and go to make up the whole. He is the human-est preacher in the world, and like Jesus, he understands the value of homely illustration, and the force that can be conveyed by gentle sarcasm.

One of his strongest points last night was illustrated by a ridiculous description of the oldtime " spare bedroom," that cold, formal and nightmare breeding atrocity of the " hospitality " of our fathers. The audience fairly ached with laughter, but the evangelist's lesson was impressed as profoundly as if he had thundered anathemas all the while; for after he had made the vision of that fearsome old spare bedroom complete, he suddenly turned upon church members of the merely formal kind, and told them:

"You have let Jesus in? Yes, but you have put Him in the spare room. You don't want Him in the rooms where you live. Take Him down into the living room. Take Him into the dining room. Take Him into the parlor. Take Him into the kitchen. Live with Him. Make Him one of the family."

Then followed a Sundayesque description of how Jesus would find beer in the refrigerator and throw it out. How He would find cards on the table and throw them out. How He would find nasty music on the piano and throw it out. How he would find cigarettes and throw them out.

"If you haven't Jesus in the rooms you live in, it's because you don't want Him," he said. "You're afraid of one of two things: You're afraid because of the things He'll throw out if He comes in, or you're afraid because of the things He'll bring with Him if He comes in."—*Times, McKeesport, Pa.*

————

Sunday was talking on Peter's preaching at Pentecost, having read these verses from the second chapter of Acts: "Others mocking said, These men are full of new wine. But Peter standing up with the eleven, lifted up his voice, and said unto them: Ye men of Judea, and all ye that dwell at Jerusalem, be this known unto you, and hearken to my words: for these are not drunken as ye suppose, seeing it is but the third hour of the day."

"The devil has been gaining on this wicked old world ever since Peter said those words. Peter couldn't use that argument now. 'They're drunk!' said the loafers, looking on. 'Drunk nothing,' said Peter. 'They're not drunk. Why, look at the time! It's only about nine o'clock. Nobody gets drunk in the morning nowadays. It will be two thousand years before men get so rotten they will take to drinking before breakfast, and to swilling booze all the morning, and to staying drunk twenty-four hours in the day. No; you're off; away off. They're not drunk. They're filled with the Spirit of God.' If Peter could come back, and the same thing were to happen, how do you like the thought that he would have to find a new argument?"

———

"To one who has not attended a Billy Sunday revival," said the *American Magazine,* some time ago, "the story of the methods by which he achieves such great results seems almost incredible. But by his works you must know him. In cold type, some of his sermons and prayers are of a sort to make all New England shiver with horror, and cause the ungodly to giggle. But they make converts. The converts become church members, and the army of salvation is augmented by thousands of recruits. Finicky critics must consider carefully before they deplore Billy Sunday. It has been our habit for centuries to discuss religion and the affairs of the soul in a King James vocabulary, and to depart from that custom has come to seem something like sacrilege. Billy Sunday talks to people about God and their souls just as men talk to one another six days in the week across the counter or the dinner table, or the street. Listen to a bit of a sermon of his on the devil:

"'The devil isn't anybody's fool. You can bank on that. Plenty of folks will tell you there isn't any devil. That he is just a figure of speech; a poetic personification of the sin in our natures. People who say that—

AS HE LOOKS TO-DAY.

and especially all the time-serving hypocritical ministers who say it, are liars. They are calling the holy Bible a lie. I'll believe the Bible before I'll believe a lot of time-serving, societyfied, tea-drinking, smirking preachers. No, sir! You take God's word for it, there is a devil, and a big one, too.

" ' Oh, but the devil is a smooth guy! He always was, and he is now. He is right on his job all the time, winter and summer. Just as he appeared to Christ in the wilderness, he is right here in this tabernacle now, trying to make you sinners indifferent to Christ's sacrifice for your salvation. When the invitation is given, and you start to get up, and then settle back into your seat, and say, " I guess I don't want to give way to a temporary impulse," that's the real, genuine, blazing-eyed, cloven-hoofed, forked-tailed old devil, hanging to your coat tails. He knows all your weaknesses, and how to appeal to them.

" ' He knows about you, and how you have spent sixty dollars in the last two years for tobacco, to make your home and the streets filthy, and that you haven't bought your wife a new dress in two years, because you " can't afford it." And he knows about you, and the time and money you spend on fool hats and card parties, doing what you call " getting into society," while your husband is being driven away from home by badly cooked meals, and your children are running loose on the streets, learning to be hoodlums.

" ' And he knows about you, too, sir, and what you get when you go back of the drug store prescription counter to " buy medicine for your sick baby." And he knows about you and that girl you are living with in sin. And he knows about you and the lie you told about the girl across the street, because she is sweeter and truer than you are, and the boys go to see her and keep away from you—you miserable thrower of slime, dug out of your own heart of envy—yes, indeed, the devil knows all about you.'"

————

It was the last night of the meeting, and Sunday was preaching his last sermon from the text: "And he said to-morrow."

"To-night when the last song is sung, the last prayer has been said, and we have all passed out into the night, and the lights have been switched off, and the place is dark, your chance, sinner, will be gone! If your heart is not soft before then, it is hardly likely that it will ever be so nearly won again. You say in your heart, 'To-morrow!' but at daylight the doctor's buggy may be standing at your gate, the family may be grouped around your bed, with handkerchiefs at their eyes. The doctor, turning to them, may say, 'He is gone.' The undertaker may come and do his work. The friends may come and listen to such kind words as may be spoken of you, and then, as Mr. Moody once said of a man who died in spite of his prayers, they may take you, a Christless corpse, in a Christless coffin, and lay you in a Christless grave! O friends! if the Lord would draw back the veil which is between some of you and your coffin, you would leap back in horror, to find it so near that you could reach out and touch it. But you say, 'To-morrow!'"

XIII

A PRESENT-DAY SUNDAY TABERNACLE
MEETING

YOU are a stranger in the city, have never seen one
of Sunday's meetings, and know nothing about
the man or his methods, except what rumor has
told you. The hotel clerk has been telling you so much
about how Sunday has taken the town that you are
going to-night to see and hear and judge for yourself.
From what you have heard you know that you must
go early to make sure of a seat. So you set out in good
time, you think, but when you reach the tabernacle you
find that a couple of thousand or more are there before
you, and stand waiting for the doors to open. The
throng grows rapidly, and soon becomes a surging multitude of many thousands. From what you have heard
at the hotel, you know that in the great crowd about
you are men and women of high and low estate, rich and
poor, the prominent people of the city, and the humble
and obscure. All meet on a common level here. Neither
birth, wealth nor talent makes any difference, so far as
obtaining a good seat is concerned. Sunday is continually beset with all kinds of propositions from those who
would secure reserved seats for themselves, but rejects
them all. Many would be glad to pay well for the
privilege, but money gives no man any advantage over
another at the tabernacle. Special delegations have

reservations on special nights, but no personal favors of that kind can be obtained.

While you stand waiting, you notice that the crowd about you is good-natured, for nobody finds fault or complains of discomfort. You notice, too, that every one is talking about the meeting, and from what you hear you gain further information as you wait.

At length the doors swing open, and you find yourself gathered up with the throng and rushed into the big building. A large corps of well-trained ushers are in their places—each man in charge of a rather small section—and you are astonished at the ease and promptness with which they have the surging mass under control and properly seated. As you drop into the seat that has come to you in the shuffle, and begin to look about, you find yourself going from one surprise to another. You little expected to find the scene so bright and attractive. You came looking for a great barnlike structure, as dimly lighted as a street car, but, wonder of wonders, how you did miss it!

You are in the largest room you ever saw, and the whole scene is glorious with electric light and bunting. Look where you will, the brightness dazzles you, and cheers one like the glad springtime, for Sunday found out a long while ago that God hates darkness. Trying to have a revival where you cannot see to read a hymn is like backing up hill with a heavy load, he thinks, and so he requires the tabernacle to be one of the most brilliantly lighted places in the city.

The building you have entered will seat about ten thousand, and there is standing room for two or three thousand more, all of which will soon be needed, for no Sunday campaign has ever yet been held where ample room could be provided for all who desired to attend

MR. AND MRS. SUNDAY,
HELEN, "BILLY" JR., GEORGE, PAUL.

some of the meetings. In all the history of great religious awakenings this has never been so generally true of any other evangelist.

One of the first things to arrest your attention is a long white banner, stretched over the platform, on which has been painted in the blackest kind of capital letters, almost three feet high, the startling legend—

"GET RIGHT WITH GOD!"

As you wait for the meeting to begin, you find yourself receiving more information from those on either side of you. On your right is a man with a Daniel Webster looking head and face, who tells you that he never saw anything so astonishing in all his life—never; and the red-faced woman on your left, who has a way of padding out her talk with " a-n-d," says that she never in all her born days heard such preaching as was done right there before her eyes last night.

Just then you notice a slender, medium-sized, wiry man, in a natty suit of clothes, with the vigor of youth in every move. He comes swinging down one of the cross aisles, shaking hands with the ushers, and now and then pausing a moment to bend over and speak to some one in a seat. Those around you are all alert now, and you hear many of them say—

" Here he comes! "

" That's Sunday! "

" That's him! "

" There's Billy! "

Then after he has reached the front and gone over to shake hands with the reporters, and some of the ministers, who have a lower corner of the platform to themselves, you begin to look around again, and the man at your side points out different members of the Sunday party, and tells you something of their various duties.

But the hour has come for the meeting to begin, and it starts on time, with a song service of a half-hour or more, in which the singing is full of life and enthusiasm. On the platform, rising in many tiers, is a chorus choir of several hundred voices. The singing alone is an experience you will mark with a white stone, for it can never be forgotten.

Many of the best singers of the city are in the choir, and it is doubtful if better music is ever heard in a religious meeting anywhere. You find it interesting to note how the vast congregation is affected by it. You see no inattention anywhere, and many, you notice, are deeply impressed. The director of the great chorus thoroughly understands his business, not only giving fine expression to the music, but inspiring each voice to do its best.

You have been closely watching the platform from which Mr. Sunday is to preach; on one end of which he now sits alone, and with eyes alert, sees everything all over the house. From a mental calculation you have been making, you estimate the platform to be near twenty feet long, from five to six feet high, and about eight feet wide, and later on you discover that every inch of it is needed.

Soon after being swept into the meeting, you notice that quite a large space in front has been roped off, and you ask the man at your side the reason therefor. Three or four nights each week, he tells you, a similar space is reserved for delegations from various lodges, labor unions, stores, factories, clubs and other societies. There is great strife, you learn, among all kinds of organizations for choice reservations, and some are kept for several days on the waiting list; another evidence, you think, of the unaccountable hold the meetings have on the city. You also learn that Billy gives a few minutes of special talk to each delegation, and it generally happens that many of those who occupy reserved seats go forward when the invitation is given. In one case that happened quite recently, you are told, every man in a certain lodge reservation went forward but three.

Presently you catch the " Tap—tap—tap ! " of a drumbeat, and the sound of marching feet comes to your ear. Then there is great cheering as a body of old soldiers comes down the aisle, following the flag, proudly borne by a grizzled veteran who has but one arm. The other he left at Gettysburg. Other delegations now file in, most of them with banners giving their names, and soon all the reserved space has been filled.

Sunday comes down from his high platform and greets several of the veterans, going first to the color-bearer, for the sight of the " old boys " has touched a tender place with him. His father marched away to the drumbeat, and never came back.

When all things have settled down to their former condition, the woman at your left tells you she would have reached the meeting sooner, but that she had to stop and check her baby. You regard her in speechless wonder for a moment, and then ask what she means. She is so fluent in conversational ability that it takes her quite a while to tell you, but at last you learn that no children under four can be taken into the tabernacle. And this is not because Sunday is opposed to little folks, but for the reason that it has been found best for the meeting to keep all babies out. A suitable place, convenient to the tabernacle, is therefore always provided, in which babies and small children are checked and cared for by nurses and other competent attendants, leaving their mothers free to enjoy the meeting. Every usher is charged by his chief to see that the rule in regard to small children is not broken, and yet in spite of the most careful scrutiny it sometimes happens that one gets in.

"But how old do the babies have to be before they can be checked?" you ask the woman.

"Oh, that don't make any difference at all; not a bit," she answers. "Why, there was one little mite that was only four weeks old when they first begun to check it three weeks ago, and I don't believe it's missed a single meeting yet. My baby is six months old, and I don't get to check it only four nights a week; though they would check it every night, and welcome to me, if I could only come. Dear me; how I wish I could. But when you have boarders and three other children you can't do everything you want to!"

After a few songs, in which the musical director has managed by one artful device or another to make about everybody take some part, except a solemn-faced reporter, who sits at his desk looking as if another steamer had gone down with all his friends on board, the opening prayer is made by one of the local clergy, and then the singing is resumed.

After two or three more songs, the time has come for taking the collection, a most important part of every meeting, until after all the current expenses have been provided for in this way. You are astonished at the rapidity with which the task of waiting on the great congregation is accomplished, for it is all over within five minutes. In this part of the meeting every one is expected to have a part, and from what you presently see and hear you believe that they do.

The taking of the offering is introduced by a few pertinent and good-natured remarks from Sunday, punctuated with laughter by the congregation, as he concludes with the well-understood expression—

"*Dig up!*"

You have noticed a bright new milk pan hanging on every post, and have wondered what its use might be. You are now going to find out. Each usher takes down a pan and sets it going through the rows in his section. In this way the large expense of the meeting— aggregating many thousands of dollars—is provided for. Not a dollar of this money goes to the evangelist, for all his remuneration comes from free will offerings given him on the last Sunday.

After more singing by the choir, Sunday takes his place directly back of the pulpit desk, about eighteen inches from it. His Bible lies wide open on the stand before him, and from it he reads his text. His voice seems husky, almost hoarse, but his words ring out, and reach every nook and corner of the enclosed and roofed-in acre called " the tabernacle." He stands with both hands hanging straight down, and his open palms tightly pressed against his sides. He is wearing a dark blue sack suit of two pieces, without the ghost of a wrinkle showing anywhere. Last night he wore a light gray suit of the same style, the woman tells you, and the night before that a rich brown.

As the first words of the text are announced his muscles become rigid, and then he bends backward as if about to throw a somersault. The manner of the preacher at the start is in a sense mild, and yet it is also vigorous in this, that everybody knows he is in earnest from the top of his head to the soles of his feet. He is not violent; he does not speak unduly loud; there is nothing approaching a strain in his voice. On the other hand, were it not for his hoarseness, you would say that he is speaking with perfect ease, and yet there is something about him that makes you feel that he will soon be hurling thunderbolts. As he proceeds, the conviction grows upon you that the preacher whose words have stirred you from the start, has a personality most extraordinary. You try to discover why you are already so alive with interest, and soon have to admit that you cannot. It is not so much in what is being said. It is not in the words with which the thoughts of the speaker are expressed. It is not in the manner in which the things you hear are being said. No, not in any of these; but it must be, you feel, in the strange compelling power of the personality that is back of what is being said. The man is not, in any sense you can define, so much unlike others you have seen and heard, and yet in spite of this you are forced into the conviction that he is in everything remarkably distinctive. You find your wits continually baffled in trying to solve the riddle, until you finally give it up as a hopeless task, and for the remainder of the hour devote your attention solely to what is being said.

Sunday preaches for a little more than an hour, and you listen with almost breathless interest from the first sentence to the last. Soon he quickens his pace, and both the highbrow and the woman whose baby is in the checkroom nudge you and say that he is " warming up." This is not information to you, for you can see the perspiration streaming down his face, and his collar begins to look as if it had seen better days. Soon he is raining great sledge-hammer blows upon the unoffending pulpit desk, as he drives home his points, and people near you start as if they had been shot at.

There is but one word at your command that will even remotely indicate his manner, and that word is ACTION! At one moment he is at one end of his long platform, and before you become used to seeing him there he is at the other, and then quicker than thought he bounds back to the center, giving the desk a solar plexus blow that would knock out a giant. Ever and anon he makes long rapid strides to give it more whacks, until at last a big piece splits off and bounds to the sawdust floor below, at which every small boy in the front row jumps and says—

" Gee ! "

Soon the preacher's face is hot and red and streaming, and the steam guage is mounting upward rapidly. As he denounces sin—and the very kind you at once recognize as your own—his eyes fairly blaze. He goes on, in a way that can only be described as awful, to picture the fate of the unrepentant sinner, and you feel that you know just how the old Hebrew prophets looked. There is no " in a degree," " to some extent " or " as it were " business about the hell that Billy Sunday preaches. He pulls off the lid so that you can almost feel the fire and smell the smoke and hear the gnashing of teeth, and charges you to remember that it was not made for you, but was prepared for the devil and his angels, and that Almighty God is doing His best to keep you from rolling into it.

You begin to understand why Sunday is so tremendously in earnest in his evangelistic efforts, and why he must keep on the go from year's end to year's end without rest, in the nerve-racking way you have witnessed. It is because he goes into the Bible for his preaching, and believes every word of his own sermon as certainly as the fearless old Tishbite believed that fire would fall from heaven just as he had declared it would.

Were it not for his unswerving belief that the statements of the Bible have come as direct from the God above us as the rain and snow come down from the clouds, and that the prophecies that have not already been fulfilled will be fulfilled to the letter, Billy Sunday would have been swept down long ago, by the principalities and powers of evil that have from the beginning of his religious career been doing their very worst against him.

But the wonderful sermon is ended. The preacher leans over his much-abused desk, seemingly limp and exhausted, and as you glance about you see a pallor on many faces. The conclusion comes abruptly, with a prayer that power shall be given to the message spoken, and that many will repent and turn to Christ. This prayer is the signal to the ushers to quietly clear the first rows of seats in front of the platform, and then as it is finished, Sunday, in a tone marked by strong feeling, says:

"You know that God has spoken to you. You know that without Christ you are lost, and that with him you are saved. You know your duty and your privilege; and now without another word from me, and before any one can have a chance to say anything to you, how many of you will settle the great question without the delay of another minute, by coming forward to take me by the hand, and by doing so confess and accept Jesus Christ as your personal Saviour? Who will come?"

What seems to be a long pause follows, but it is less than thirty seconds, and then, half-way down the aisle, a man rises and walks quickly toward the front. Before he has gone twenty paces a woman, with streaks of gray

her hair, edges her way out into the aisle and follows,
d then come two little girls and four men, one of
hom is the one-armed veteran who carried the flag.
ow they have started in another aisle, and so they
llow each other in solemnity and quiet, for there is no
nging, until several score have gone forward. Then
ere is a lull, and the personal workers are told to go
t. They quickly and quietly scatter all over the house.
ree more of the veterans go forward, and in ones
d twos and threes and fours, and then in larger
oups down all the aisles seekers begin to move, and
they thus move forward the preacher's face fairly
ines.

There is singing now, and it is continued until all
ho will have come, the ushers meantime skillfully keep-
g the aisles open, and the request is made that no one
all leave the building at this stage of the meeting.

Three rows clear across the central section have been
led, and then four, and now five, and still they come.
hen after another row or two is filled, Sunday gives
ose before him clear instruction as to how to make
eir beginning in Christian life. Then he prays that
ey may be divinely helped and guided; find the right
urch home, and have grace to meet every obligation
d duty as Christian men, women and children.

The secretaries have them sign the decision cards,
ving their names, street address and church prefer-
ce. While this is going on the city pastors are on
eir honor not to approach any one until the cards have
en signed. There is then a great deal of handshaking,
d by this the meeting is generally dismissed without
formal benediction. While the last song is being sung,
unday, who is wet to the skin, from his hour of more
an strenuous exertion, puts on his overcoat and stands

leaning over the pulpit desk looking down upon the busy scene before him. It is near ten o'clock, but he is a poor sleeper, and seldom retires before midnight.

The foregoing is a true picture, and typical of the many mammoth meetings that are held each year.

"BE IT EVER SO HUMBLE, THERE'S NO PLACE LIKE HOME."

XIV

SPECIAL FEATURES CONNECTED WITH THE SUNDAY MEETINGS

SUNDAY'S corps of helpers consists of nearly a dozen people, made up of both men and women. His wife is with him most of the time in nearly every meeting, and she is of course his best helper.

In general, arrangements are made so that the men of the party can live together under one roof, and so keep up something of home life. The ladies generally have rooms in homes near by, so that all can have meals at the same table. It is also an advantage in many ways, for them to be close together. Whenever it can be done, the Executive Committee rents a large furnished house, and employs a housekeeper and other needed help. When this is not done, Sunday finds it difficult to get the time he needs for rest and work. His correspondence alone is heavy and burdensome, for although he has a most efficient secretary, so much of it requires his own personal attention.

In connection with the great meetings are many special features that require skilled supervision and constant oversight, and no little downright hard work on the part of every member of the party. The first and most important of these are the cottage prayer meetings, about a hundred or more of which are held, in the larger places, every morning at ten o'clock.

These are the spiritual life of the great meetings. To

have them go on successfully and profitably is no small task, and in this the local pastors can give much help. The city is divided into districts of a few blocks each, in every one of which a prayer meeting is held daily. The aim is to have these meetings held in different homes each morning, and not in the same ones continuously. There is also a daily change in the leaders. In the choosing of leaders care must be taken, not only to have those who will be spiritual and competent, but who will also be prompt and punctual, and see that the meetings begin and close on time. It has been found an advantage to hold as many of these meetings as possible in the homes of non-Christians.

Another feature that has much to do with the success of the great meetings is the holding of meetings in shops and factories during the noon hour. The men in the shops take much interest in these meetings, and are glad to have them as often as they can be held. At each one there is good singing and a short address, made by Sunday or one of his assistants. Sometimes meetings are also held for the clerks in the larger stores. Numerous meetings are held in the schools, and Sunday's educational talks are among the best and most practical he gives. By them many young lives have been turned into better channels.

One very important special feature is the work that is done among women of several classes: Business women, factory girls, maids, society women, wives, mothers, schoolgirls, etc. One of Sunday's women assistants holds meetings for the business women—stenographers, clerks, bookkeepers, etc., in which they are organized into classes and given special help and instruction in Bible study and other matters pertaining to young women. These meetings are held during the noon hour, and luncheon is provided for them three days in the week. The attendance upon these runs from four hundred to a thousand daily, according to size of city.

Another young woman assistant holds meetings at noontime in factories, and with the maids at a different hour on another day, and so with girls of other classes who support themselves.

Another woman assistant has had large experience as a Bible teacher, and does a very much needed work in her line, by organizing wives, mothers, housekeepers and all others she can enlist, into classes for a systematic study of the Scriptures, and under her skillful training a most enthusiastic interest is soon awakened in the study of the Bible, which continues for years after the meetings have been held. This assistant often returns for a few days, to give the classes any renewed help that may be needed.

In one city where a meeting was in progress a traveling man went into his hotel, and with a look of amazement on his face, said to the clerk:

" I just saw the strangest sight I ever saw in my life."

" And what was it?" said the clerk, as he jabbed a pen into the glass of shot.

" Why, it was more than a hundred women passing along the sidewalk, and every last one of them was carrying a Bible!"

And this shows what a marked impression such Bible work as Sunday is having done must have on a community.

The lady above referred to also forms personal workers classes and trains them to do intelligent and effective personal work in the meetings and elsewhere. Many so trained become real soul winners.

She also meets the high school girls three times a week, and gives them practical instruction in Bible study. She plans and arranges for meetings of women in homes, arranges group meetings, etc., and herself addresses many women's meetings.

The gospel is not only preached to the poor in the tabernacle, and carried to the unfortunate in many ways that appeal to them through the various channels of the Sunday meetings, but special efforts are also made to reach the wealthy. Meetings especially for this class are also held in the homes of society people, where for the time the ballroom is turned into a chapel, and some of the best preaching Sunday has ever done he does here. In no other meeting does he have a more attentive hearing, or preach more impressively.

The place is always crowded with women who move in the upper circles, many of whom never heard a straight-out gospel sermon from a man who had the courage to speak the truth as it is given in the Bible. These people have found by experience that wealth and high station can never satisfy an immortal spirit, and in their souls many of them have long yearned for something better. Many who thus hear the truth in the homes of friends want more of it, and so become attendants at the tabernacle. Sunday was the first evangelist to undertake this most important and sadly neglected work.

In wide contrast to this, meetings are also held in jails and prisons. When holding meetings in Columbus, Ohio, where the State Penitentiary is located, Mr. Sunday held services in the great prison every Wednesday and Sabbath morning, at nine o'clock, and hundreds of the prisoners were converted, and since their release have lived upright lives. His Bible teachers had a class of over eight hundred in the prison, and the men were taught the word of God.

Another marked feature is the mammoth men's meetings that are held almost every Sunday afternoon in the tabernacle, and which is always filled to its fullest capacity. The attendance at these meetings is so unprecedented that no matter how great the capacity of the building may be, it is always crowded to the utmost, and thousands are turned away.

No one can have the remotest idea of how men can be stirred, until he has attended one of these great meetings. In them multitudes have taken their stand for Christ, and other thousands of men whose names had long been on church rolls have been changed from lukewarmness and indifference into live wires of Christian energy. Whenever a large number have to be turned away from any of the tabernacle meetings, an overflow meeting is held in the largest accessible church, conducted by Sunday's assistants.

While meetings for men only are being held at the tabernacle, from one to three meetings for women only are held, addressed by Mrs. Sunday and other ladies of the party, and these meetings are always larger in attendance than the capacity of the churches in which they are held can accommodate. A great many conversions have taken place in them.

Another great meeting is one for women alone, where Sunday makes an address especially for women, and which no man has ever yet been allowed to attend. Not even the musical director, Sunday's first assistant or the janitor can remain. Unprincipled men have sometimes tried to smuggle themselves in, but have soon been discovered and ousted. Not a great while ago two young fellows in women's apparel attempted it, but Mrs. Sunday was acting as chief usher just then, and her quick eye detected them. She walked over to them, and put out her hand to shake hands. When they stretched out their big paws her suspicions were confirmed, and very much crestfallen they were shown to the door, getting a good deal tangled up in their hobble skirts as they stampeded toward the exit. In some of these meetings hundreds of well-dressed women have sat down on the shavings in the aisles and open spaces, while other thousands were unable to get into the building.

The meeting for women only, during the campaign in Columbus, Ohio, was perhaps the most wonderful ever held in America. The hour for the service to commence had been announced for two o'clock, but at five o'clock in the morning women began to gather about the building, waiting for the doors to open. By ten o'clock twelve thousand women were packed in the building, every available foot of space being taken. Hundreds were clamoring to get in, and every street car was packed, bringing thousands more. Automobiles rushed up with their precious loads of elegantly gowned women from the homes of the rich, all wild to gain an entrance.

Word being sent to Mr. Sunday, he hurried to the tabernacle, and announced that he would preach to those already in the building. They would then pass out through the rear doors, and those waiting outside would be admitted, and the sermon repeated to them. This announcement was greeted with wild cheers. When the doors were opened twelve thousand women swept in, brushing the police to one side as though they were children.

Sunday finished the sermon the second time at three-thirty; rushed to his hotel; changed his clothes, which were dripping wet from perspiration; jumped into an automobile and hurried to the Ohio State University, where he addressed two thousand students, assembled in the great gymnasium. Then back home for a few minutes rest. Then again hurrying to the tabernacle to preach the same sermon to twelve thousand business women—from office, factory, shop and store—who had been given special tickets of admission. In all, nearly forty thousand different women attended the services in one day, and thus closed the most remarkable demonstration of the kind ever seen in the United States.

This is what a lady of South Bend had to say in one of the local papers, concerning the Woman's Meeting there:

" Billy Sunday's talk to women was a plain talk on a plain subject, and as Billy said, he was ' bitterly maligned' by those whom he calls ' foul-mouthed degenerates,' when they say his sermon is shocking. In my opinion every word of that sermon should be put in print, and then cut out and put in a woman's scrapbook of choice clippings. He talked plain, but if plain talk was ever needed it is needed to-day. Nothing else will ever make some women stop and think. The power of his personality is shown when something unusual causes a stir in the audience. Last night a restless movement was noticed once, and the whole audience and I held our breath, for I knew one scream, one false move, and thousands of women would be turned into so many wildcats fighting for their lives. But Billy spoke a word of assurance, and quiet was restored. The meeting was a wonderful gathering of women, and its like will never be seen in South Bend again. As a woman observer it did me a world of good, and ' it was good to have been there.' "

Another great special feature of the campaign is the day that is set apart for mothers. On this day everybody in the city is urged to wear a white carnation, white flower of some kind, or if the flower is not obtainable, a white ribbon in memory of mother. Acts of kindness that would please mother, are urged upon every one for that day. If she is living, write her a good letter, or send her some flowers.

"If your mother is dead, it is requested that you remember what she was to you. Recall how great has been her influence upon you for good; thank God that you had a good mother, and say again the prayer she taught you. If your mother is dead, do an act of kindness to somebody else's mother. If you have an auto or a carriage, use it, or give its use to carry old mothers to the tabernacle."

The day meeting that day is called "Mother's Meeting." The songs "mother used to sing" are sung, and the sermon by Mr. Sunday is very tender and very touching, and is especially addressed to mothers. The influence of the day can never be forgotten by those who attend the meetings. In many cities the stores and factories close during the hours of the meeting.

Among the most important features is the Sunday school parade, which usually takes place about the third week of the meeting, and in which about all the schools in the county participate. People always look for something much out of the ordinary in this parade, and yet when it is seen they are much more than astonished— they are amazed.

At Wilkes-Barre, Pa., where perhaps the largest thus far held took place, it was estimated that fully twenty thousand were in line, and that at least thirty thousand more turned out to witness the wonderful event. The

LIVING ROOM AND DINING ROOM IN HOME AT WINONA
LAKE, IND.

procession was four miles long, marching four, and
sometimes eight abreast. It took an hour and twenty-two
minutes to pass a given point, including stops. The
illustrations on other pages give but a faint idea of it.
It was in April, and the weather ideal. The following
account of it is from the Wilkes-Barre *Record:*

"Circus days in the palmiest period of their pros-
perity never proved more magnetic in drawing people
to the city. Every car the traction company could press
into service was employed in handling the enormous sub-
urban traffic. The summer cars were brought out, and
every one packed to the limit. The people making up
the various delegations began to assemble on the river
common as early as ten o'clock. At noon it was almost
impossible to move on River street, and at the Market
street bridge the scene presented would have rivaled
that in a metropolitan city on election night. No attempt
was made at formation until the parade started to move.
This occurred promptly to the minute scheduled.

"Mr. Sunday appeared about three minutes ahead of
time, walking from the Sterling with Mrs. Sunday, his
self-confessed commander-in-chief. Promptly at twelve-
thirty he gave the signal to the chief marshal, and the
column started. The bands commenced to play, and the
ranks fell into step. A platoon of mounted police kept
the way clear. A car containing a number of women,
members of the evangelistic party, formed the vanguard.
Mr. and Mrs. Sunday, and most of the members of the
party, marched in the procession.

"Everywhere the marchers advanced they were
greeted with the same intense enthusiasm that marked the
whole demonstration. At one point the mayor was
picked up, loaded into a car and taken along. Traffic
along the route of march was blocked for about two

hours. The makeup of the parade was something different from anything ever seen in our city.

" The main body of the column was composed of children, although there were thousands of adults in line. Numerous auto trucks and heavy wagons punctuated the line at various points. They were loaded with tiny children too small to march. Nearly every one who participated carried a banner or flag of some kind. Two sprinklers mounted by crowds of little youngsters made literal water wagons, and the fact was emblazoned on cards that admonished every one to ' Cut out Booze! ' Hay wagons, carts, autos of all kinds carried hundreds of the little tots.

" The scene at the tabernacle after the parade was one that cannot soon be forgotten. The vast building was packed to the doors with an audience made up mostly of children, and Sunday preached a sermon especially to them. Four buildings were packed. The tabernacle with seven to eight thousand; a church seating over two thousand, and in Majestic Theater were packed fifteen hundred more. Beside this, another meeting was held in one of the churches. All the meetings were addressed by members of the Sunday party. By this time it was scarcely four o'clock, and the parade disbanded with thousands who were unable to get into a meeting, some of whom had been marching since twelve-thirty.

" When it was suggested in the tabernacle that the Sunday school parade be made an annual event, the entire audience leaped to their feet in acclamation of the proposal."

The wildest kinds of rumors, reports, charges and slanders are in circulation as to the ironclad requirements that must be met before Sunday will engage to hold a meeting in any city, and one of the basest of these is that he requires a money guarantee of twenty thousand dollars for his services. This is absolutely false, and has not a single word of truth in it. He never has made any requirement on this line whatever, except that he shall receive what the people will voluntarily give him on the last Sunday of the meeting. He makes no stipulation whatever as to the amount he shall receive.

Sunday takes a deep interest in the spiritual well-being of those who take a stand for Christ in his meetings, and aims to have them clearly and intelligently understand the meaning of the step they take. Individual cases, that for some particular reason are brought to his attention, he sometimes keeps in touch with for years. A carefully prepared leaflet, the result of years of experience, study and prayer, is presented to each one at the time the stand is taken. It reads as follows:

DEAR FRIEND: You have by this act of coming forward publicly acknowledged your faith in Jesus Christ as your personal Saviour. No one could possibly be more rejoiced that you have done this, or be more anxious for you to succeed and get the most joy and service out of the Christian life than I. I therefore ask you to read carefully this little tract. Paste it in your Bible and read it frequently.

What It Means to be a Christian.—A Christian is any man, woman or child who comes to God as a lost sinner, accepts the Lord Jesus Christ as his personal Saviour, surrenders to Him as his Lord and Master; confesses Him as such before the world, and strives to please Him in everything, day by day.

Have *you* come to God realizing that *you* are a lost

sinner? Have *you* accepted the Lord Jesus Christ as *your* personal Saviour? That is, do *you* believe with all your heart that God laid all *your* iniquity on Him? (Isa. 53:5-6). And that He bore the penalty of *your* sins (1 Pet. 2:24) and that your sins are forgiven because Jesus died in your stead?

Have *you* surrendered to Him as your Lord and Master? That is, are you willing to do His will, even when it conflicts with your desire?

Have *you* confessed Him as your Saviour and Master before the world?

Is it your purpose to strive to please Him in everything day by day?

If *you* can sincerely answer *"Yes"* to the foregoing questions, then you may know, on the authority of God's word, that *you* are *now* a child of God (John 1:12); that you have *now* eternal life (John 3:36); that is to say, if you have done your part (i.e., believe that Christ died in your place, and receive Him as your Saviour and Master), God has done *His* part, and imparted to you His own nature (2 Peter 1:4).

How to Make a Success of the Christian Life.—Now that you are a child of God, *your* growth depends upon yourself.

It is impossible for you to become a useful Christian unless you are willing to do the things which are absolutely essential to your spiritual growth. To this end the following suggestions will be found to be of vital importance:

Study the Bible.—Set aside at least fifteen minutes a day for Bible study. Let God talk to you fifteen minutes a day through His Word. Talk to God fifteen minutes a day in prayer. Talk for God fifteen minutes a day.

As newborn babes desire the sincere milk of the word, that ye may grow thereby.—1 Peter 2:2.

The word of God is food for the soul. Commit to memory one verse of Scripture each day. Join a Bible class (Ps. 119:11).

Pray Much.—Praying is talking to God. Talk to Him about everything—your perplexities, joys, sorrows, sins, mistakes, friends, enemies, etc.

Be careful for nothing; but in everything by prayer and supplication with thanksgiving let your requests be made known unto God.—Phil. 4:6.

Win Some One for Christ.—For spiritual growth you need not only food (Bible study), but exercise. Work for Christ. The only work Christ ever set for Christians is to win others.

Go ye into all the world, and preach the gospel to every creature.—Mark 16:15.

When I say unto the wicked, Thou shalt surely die; and thou givest him not warning, nor speakest to warn the wicked from his wicked way, to save his life; the same wicked man shall die in his iniquity; but his blood will I require at thine hand.—Ezek. 3:18.

Shun Evil Companions.—Avoid bad people, bad books, bad thoughts. Read the first psalm.

Be ye not unequally yoked together with unbelievers: for what fellowship hath righteousness with unrighteousness? and what communion hath light with darkness? or what part hath he that believeth with an infidel? Wherefore come out from among them, and be ye separate, saith the Lord.—2 Cor. 6:14-17.

Try to win the wicked for God, but do not choose them for your companions.

Join Some Church.—Be faithful in your attendance at the Sabbath and mid-week services.

> Not forsaking the assembling of ourselves together, as the manner of some is.—Heb. 10:25.

Co-operate with Your Pastor.—God has appointed the pastor to be a shepherd over the church, and you should give him due reverence, and seek to assist him in his plans for the welfare of the church.

Give to the Support of the Lord's Work.—Give as the Lord hath prospered you (1 Cor. 16:2).

> Give not grudgingly or of necessity, for God loveth a cheerful giver.—2 Cor. 9:7.

Do Not Become Discouraged.—Expect temptations, discouragement and persecution. The Christian life is a warfare.

> Yea, and all that will live godly in Christ Jesus shall suffer persecution.—2 Tim. 3:12.

" The eternal God is thy refuge." We have the promise that all things, even strange, hard and unaccountable obstacles, work together for our good. Many of God's brightest saints who were once as weak as you are, passed through dark tunnels and the hottest fires, and

MR. AND MRS. SUNDAY ON THE GOLF LINKS.

yet their lives were enriched by their experiences, and
the world was made better because of their having lived
in it.

Read often the following passages of Scripture:
Romans 8:18; James 1:12; 1 Cor. 10:13.

Near the close of each campaign a Personal Workers'
League is organized, to aid the churches in maintaining
the revival spirit after the meetings end. In some places
hundreds of names are enrolled, and in the list will be
representatives from all classes converted at the tabernacle, and others who have for years been church members. These Leaguers stand pledged to hold up the
hands of their pastor, and stand shoulder to shoulder
with him in all his endeavors to make religion something
more than a name. They give life to the prayer and
other devotional meetings of their own church, and also
to the Sunday school and adult Bible classes.

Teams are also organized among them for aggressive
evangelistic work, and by them meetings are held in their
own and neighboring communities. They hold noon
meetings, in shops, factories, etc., and make all possible
effort to get men to take an interest in religion. By
such efforts a revival spirit is maintained, and hundreds
of people are converted. At Youngstown, Ohio, for instance, where Sunday held a meeting in 1908, the revival
fires have been kept burning in the churches ever since.
The gains in church membership have been not only
steady, but surprising.

Through the personal workers at Wichita, Kan.,
where Sunday held a meeting in 1911, nineteen hundred
and thirteen men and boys were reported converted
within a year from the close of the campaign. Also

through the example and influence of the Wichita workers, converts in other towns organized similar teams, and extended the work into other districts. A moment's thought will show what a power for good a live Personal Workers' League may become in any community.

XV

SOME OF SUNDAY'S SAYINGS

BETTER limp all the way to heaven than not get there at all.

To make seeking God the first business of life, is to begin right.

In the sight of God there is no difference between being wrong and doing wrong.

If you would be taken over the river dry-shod, you must get into the boat.

I would rather have standing room in heaven· than own the world and go to hell.

If good preaching could save the world, it would have been done long ago.

The man who can drive a hog and keep his religion, will stand without hitching.

The inconsistency is not in the Bible, but in your life.

There are men in hell because they wasted too much time in trying to find out where Cain got his wife.

You can find everything in the average church, from a humming bird to a turkey buzzard.

The man who sneers at true religion turns up his nose at one of the best things on earth.

You don't have to look like a hedgehog to be pious.

Riches have never yet given anybody either peace or rest.

If there is no hell, a good many preachers are obtaining money under false pretenses.

The man who is right with God will not be wrong with anything that is good.

Some of the biggest lies ever told are to be found on gravestones.

In every community are some folks the devil can catch with a bare hook.

If you depend on your emotions for motive power, you will come to a good many places where the wires won't work.

The Bible will always be full of things you cannot understand, as long as you will not live according to those you can understand.

God never says no to the man who is really in earnest.

Don't stop with telling your boy to do right. Show him how.

Better die an old maid, sister, than marry the wrong man.

Our homes are on a level with our women.

The devil has a mortgage on many a child from the day it is born.

You never hear of a man marrying a woman to reform her.

Is there any bread in rum? Yes, for the brewer and the saloon keeper, but not for the drunkard's family.

There are too many men in the pulpit to-day who preach as if they didn't expect any help from God.

Going to church don't make anybody a Christian, any more than taking a wheelbarrow into a garage makes it an automobile.

There never was a doubt in the world that didn't come straight from the devil.

No hypocrite in the church, or out of it, is going to get into heaven.

If you live as God wants you to your life will have some lines in it like those in the face of Christ.

Too many churches are little more than four walls and a roof.

I would rather be pastor of a graveyard than of some churches.

The right preaching of the gospel will never hurt anything good.

The big bugs in the church are mistaken about as often as the little ones.

The man who votes for the saloon is pulling on the same rope with the devil, whether he knows it or not.

God pity the country when the devil gets the home.

To have to live with some people is to slide toward the pit.

A decent man ought to be ashamed to live in a town that is run by the devil's gang.

Call the devil by his right name, and you will make many a man with broad phylacteries as mad as fire.

You can have as many theories as you please, but you will never get into heaven unless you plant your feet on the Rock of Ages.

If you would have your children turn out well, don't turn your home into a lunch counter and lodging house.

Trying to run a church without revivals can be done— when you can run a gasoline engine on buttermilk.

If the womanhood of America had been no better than its manhood, the devil would have had the country fenced in long ago.

Some homes need a hickory switch a good deal more than they do a piano.

The devil hates the church, but he likes the work some highbrows do in it.

Some of the biggest rooms in hell will be crowded full of church members.

Many a man who is rolling down hill faster than a fox can run, will tell you that he is on his way to heaven.

Enthusiasm is as good a thing in religion as fire is in a cook stove.

When I hit the devil square in the face some people go away as mad as if I had slapped them in the mouth.

The man who has no passion for souls is liable to get mad at the drop of a hat.

Man was a fool in the Garden of Eden, and he has taken a good many new degrees since.

There are some homes that never hurt the devil's business.

The backslider likes the preaching that wouldn't hit the side of a house, while the real disciple is delighted when the truth brings him to his knees.

The man who don't believe in a hell is about sure to be scorching to it with both pedals loose.

Some preachers preach as if all their members were saints.

The devil will say amen to the preaching that says the world is becoming better and better.

Don't throw any mud at the plan of salvation until you try it and find out that it won't work.

Whenever the devil gets a chance to put a thorn in a good man's side, he jabs it in deep.

No photographer could make a living taking pictures, if he made them look just like you.

Look into the preaching Jesus did, and you will find it was aimed straight at the big sinners on the front seats.

The repentance that counts with God must be brought down to a spot cash basis.

There would be more power in the prayers of some folks if they would put more white money in the collection basket.

There wouldn't be so many non-church goers if there were not so many non-going churches.

Be careful, father, or while you are making one lap around the devil's track your boy will make six.

God keeps no half-way house. It's either heaven or hell for you and me.

If there is a heaven for fools, the man who thinks he can get to glory on his wife's religion will be there on a front seat.

Not to walk in the straight and narrow way yourself, is to give the devil the biggest kind of a chance to get your children.

If you follow some of the star preachers you will be lost in the woods, but if you follow Christ you will be sure to land in heaven.

If you are strangers to prayer you are strangers to power.

When picking out a man's coffin, the worst thing to say about him is that he had no enemies.

The devil never put a wickeder lie into the heart of any man, than that the way to be a Christian is to be solemn and cold and sour.

I am not the author of the plan of salvation, but I am responsible for the way I preach it.

The world needs the best you can give it.

The father who keeps his boy away from school is doing his best to make a fool out of him.

Not how well you have done, but how what you have done compares with what you might have done is what counts.

What you have given the world it never possessed before you came.

The difference between God's side and the devil's is the difference between heaven and hell.

Temptation is not sin—yielding is.

A man can slip into hell with his hand on the door knob of heaven.

Ball bearings on the church doors will never fill the pews with sinners seeking salvation.

Temptation is the devil looking through the keyhole. Yielding is opening the door and inviting him in.

If you live wrong you can't die right.

To discover a flaw in our makeup is a chance to get rid of it, and add a new line of beauty to our life.

God will not send the winds to drive our ship of salvation, unless we have faith to lift the sails.

The real man shuns a path carpeted with velvet.

If you are going to be carried over the rough places you might as well have no legs at all.

All the service that weighs an ounce in the sight of God is that which is prompted by love.

I am an old-fashioned preacher of the old-time religion, that has warmed this cold world's heart for two thousand years.

To know some men is an invitation to do right. To know others is an invitation to lie, drink, swear and sink into hell.

What God needs, and the world needs, is men who are solid mahogany all the way through.

XVI

SUNDAY'S HOME AND OTHER FAMILY
AFFAIRS

M R. SUNDAY'S mother is still living, and only a
mother can know and appreciate the great joy
and satisfaction she has had in hearing her son
preach to vast multitudes with such marvelous power,
and seeing him so wondrously used of God in the saving
of many. It has been her privilege to have a seat on the
platform in many of his great meetings, and there witness
scenes that melted her heart in gratitude.

Sunday has always been glad to have his mother with
him at the tabernacle whenever she could be present,
and has had his heart made very tender by the heartiness
of the applause that always greeted her whenever he
introduced her. God has a thousand ways of pouring
the oil of joy into the heart of a mother, and to this
Sunday's mother can abundantly testify.

Billy's love for his mother, and his intense loyalty to
her, has been a grand example to thousands of young
people all over the country and this has always reached
the climax of influence in every campaign when the special " Mothers' Day " services were held.

Everything in the way of good that comes to Sunday
he is proud and happy to share with his wife. Next
to the favor of God, it is doubtful if there is anything
more precious to him than " Nell's " smile of enjoyment,
and she is just as glad when the dew of heaven comes

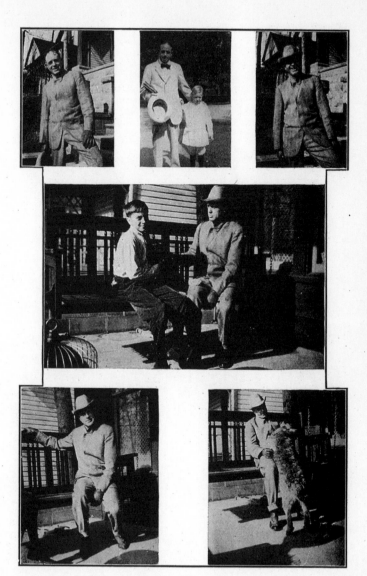

AS HE APPEARS AT HOME, BETWEEN MEETINGS.

to him. Along with the great honors and tributes that are bestowed upon Sunday in the cities where he goes, Mrs. Sunday must be at his side to share them if she is anywhere near.

If she is on the platform behind him when any special ovation or present is offered him, a glance in her direction, and a characteristic jerk of his head is a wireless signal that is by the whole multitude instantly understood, and it promptly brings her to his side. This noble example from a leader so prominent cannot but have a most wholesome influence in many a home.

A short time ago, Mr. Sunday's youngest boy—little Paul, a six-year-old—had the experience that is always so momentous to the small boy—his first day in school.

He had for some time been looking forward to it as being a fine thing to have to do, but when the day at last really dawned, it was quite a solemn thing for little Paul. There was no smile on his bright little face that morning, and for once in his life he was actually still. There is good ground for believing that he might have backed out altogether but for Willie, who braced him up as one boy knows so well how to help another.

Willie is Paul's hero, for Willie is twelve, and that makes him quite a giant to his baby brother. He is all, and mayhap more to Paul than Simon Peter was to Andrew. He always feels safe when Willie is close by, and is never timid about following Willie anywhere. He would follow him into the lions' den.

Had Jonah had a younger brother with him on the ship, who believed in him as little Paul does in Willie, the whale would have had to carry two passengers instead of one, and think of the extra trouble that would have made for some of the Bible critics.

But little Paul's first day at school came and went, as

all other days are certain to do, and that evening his
mother had a little talk with him about his new experience.

" Tell me all about it, Paul," said his mother. " How
did you get along? "

" I didn't get along at all," was the reply.

" Why, Paul, what do you mean by that? What did
you do? "

" Didn't do nothing! "

" Didn't do anything? Child, what do you mean? I
want to know all about it."

" They didn't give me nothing to do; only to just sit
there. And I can't waste my time that way," said little
Paul, who from his father's incessant activity seems to
think that not to be doing something with all your might
is a most sinful waste of the golden moments.

By the way, the very day on which Paul was born
his father had to leave home to begin a meeting at Gibson
City, Ill. Paul was born at seven-thirty in the morning,
and an hour later Mr. Sunday had to grab up his suitcase
and make a dash for the railroad depot, without stopping
to even form a speaking acquaintance with the boy.

When Willie was born the situation was even less de-
sirable, for Sunday was up to his eyes in a meeting at
Harlan, Iowa, and didn't get to see the new baby until
it was ten days old, and had taken command of the entire
household.

This shows how little an evangelist is able to control
his own movements or consult his own feelings. The
importance of the work in which he is engaged is so
great and far reaching, and the interests at stake so
widespread and multitudinous, and his own personal and
family affairs of such slight consequence in comparison,
that he must anoint his altar with the blood of sacrifice,

and go straight on in the line of duty, no matter how trying or difficult he may find the task.

Willie has always been a natural born explorer. Almost from the cradle he has shown a tendency to investigate that could not be suppressed. From the time he was a very little boy anything that was new and strange was like the call of the wild to him. He could no more be kept from trying to investigate than Lieut. Peary could be kept from trying to reach the North Pole.

Every town to which Willie went with his parents was a new world that he was as eager to explore as Columbus was to discover America. In making the rounds of the stores with his father's party, he was always slipping away to make side explorations on his own account. The singular thing about it is that he could find his way and keep his bearings like a greyhound, and was never lost. He would turn up again when least expected. He would glide from counter to counter, and from floor to floor until he had covered the plant, and then he was ready to go to another place.

When Willie was about six years old Mr. Sunday went to visit his assistant, in another part of the city, taking the boy along. While the men were talking the little fellow went all over the house, from cellar to attic, and came into the room through a door that the occupant himself had not previously noticed.

After a day or two in a new town the little chap could go anywhere alone. Had not the North and South Poles been already discovered, it is almost certain that Willie would sooner or later have found them both.

Both Willie and Paul were born on the same day of the week, and the same day of the month. Willie was born on Saturday, June 15, 1901, and Paul on Saturday, June 15, 1907.

Helen was born on January 29, 1890, while her father was still playing ball. She is married, and lives at Elmhurst, near Chicago. She is now Mrs. Mark P. Haines.

George was born November 12, 1892, while his father was Secretary of the Religious Department of the Chicago Y. M. C. A. His full name is George Marquis, the latter name being in honor of an old pastor of the family. George is also married.

The Sundays first began housekeeping in Chicago at 700 Monroe street, in a four-room flat. Here they lived two years, and until after Helen was born. They then removed to a larger flat, at 64 Throop street, and here their other three children were born. This continued to be their home until 1910, when they built their present home at Winona Lake, Ind. They had, however, had a summer cottage there for something like ten years before this.

The South Bend *Tribune* published an article giving the following information:

"A slender man, roughly dressed in old clothes, was at work on the hillside lawn in front of the cozy home of Billy Sunday, at Winona Lake, one day when a couple of visitors called to see the famous baseball evangelist. They were newspaper men from South Bend, sent to learn something of the home life of the Sundays.

"Is this the home of Mr. Sunday?" asked the two in chorus of the man, whom they took to be the gardener.

"Yes, he lives here," was the laconic answer, as he motioned toward the house, and scarcely raised his head.

"Who wants to see him?"

"A couple of newspaper men."

"Well, what do you want?"

"To see Mr. Sunday."

"All right; look at him. Here he is."

And as he spoke, the evangelist, who looked much more like a laboring man than a preacher, in the clothes he wore, turned half around and regarded his visitors narrowly from under the brim of a tattered hat.

" We wanted to find out something in advance concerning your meetings," one of the men suggested.

" I know of nothing," said the man in the old clothes, as he turned on his heel and walked away.

Apparently the interview was over, but it was plain after he had taken several turns up and down the lawn, that this was just one of his old habits of moving about nervously as he talks.

" How about your arrangement of sermons? " one of them queried, as he turned and approached again.

" There is none. I don't have any," and he was off again.

Again it looked as if the interview were over. Sunday displayed no further interest in his callers, and they strolled nervously about on the lawn, as he dodged here and there among the bushes and flower beds, removing dead branches and twigs that had collected during the winter.

There was a long, painful silence.

Then suddenly the wiry man straightened up, and it was here he displayed the first sign of interest.

" How are things in South Bend, anyway? " he asked, looking from one of his visitors to the other. " Do the people appear interested in the coming revival? "

" They do."

The reply undoubtedly pleased him, for when he spoke again he showed his pleasure with a broad smile.

Then there was something said about the " booze crowd " in South Bend, and the ice was broken.

Sunday spoke at length, and with his well-known vigor,

concerning the "booze crowd," his arch enemy the world over, and when he had finished his manner was entirely changed. With much animation he shouted to his wife that a couple of newspaper men had come to see them, whereupon the woman who is his guiding star, his most private secretary and all-around adviser, appeared.

Two minutes of conversation with Mr. Sunday, and as much more with his better half, would reveal to the dullest mind that she has been one of the most important factors in changing a ball player into one of the greatest evangelists of modern times.

Mr. Sunday forgets names, dates and faces, and any number of other things, and his wife remembers them for him. He forgets where he puts important telegrams and other papers, and she finds them for him. He calls her to do this, and asks her about that, and with a smile that never loses its luster, she always responds.

Mrs. Sunday shook hands with the visitors with a cordial manner that spelled welcome. Then there suddenly appeared two energetic small boys, neither of which could stand still a minute. The oldest wanted his tennis racket, and the other something to eat. Their wants were supplied, and later they appeared again, with a grin that told they had not been disappointed.

"What would you say to posing for some pictures?" was asked the evangelist and Mrs. Sunday.

"It's the easiest thing I do," said he, as he threw himself into position for a snapshot on the steps of his residence.

"Daddy, you wouldn't have your picture taken in that outfit?" cried his wife, womanlike, and horrified.

"Sure. Why not?" And in "that outfit" he was taken.

The next few minutes were occupied in photographing

MR. AND MRS. SUNDAY.

the Sunday family in various places and poses. In one Billy sat in the swing fondling his valuable dog, and in another he appeared beside the cage of the family parrot. When the picture taking was completed he had become a most gracious host.

" Come in, and look through my forty-thousand dollar house," said he, laughing; " the house that cost me exactly thirty-eight hundred dollars to build."

Inside he explained the forty-thousand dollar connection with his residence.

"Mrs. Sunday and I always call it our forty-thousand dollar home," said he, " because the ' booze crowd ' have advertised it from one end of the country to the other, as having cost me that. The truth of the matter is that it cost me exactly thirty-eight hundred dollars, and I spent about a thousand dollars in addition on interior decorations. So it is an investment of just about five thousand dollars, just an eighth of the amount charged against me by the ' booze gang,' and that is about as close as they ever come to the truth in anything.

" We think we have it right cozy here," said Sunday, as he dropped into an easy chair near the door, and a better word could not be found in the dictionary to describe the Sunday home. It is cozy all over.

It is ideally planned, and so filled with pretty things that you want to ask Billy if he is ever tempted to remain at home for the balance of his life. The question unasked was answered indirectly soon afterward, when Mrs. Sunday volunteered the information that " Daddy always dreaded to leave it again after a rest there."

The entire front of the house is taken up with one large living-room, finished and furnished elegantly. It is a combination of parlor, sitting-room, den and music room. A wide hallway runs from this room to the rear of the house, and this has been turned into quite a picture gallery. On the walls hang many fine enlargements of various members of the family; oils painted by Mrs. Sunday several years ago, and other pictures of merit and interest.

The house has two stories, and astonishes you at the number of good-sized rooms it contains. There are several bedchambers and two sleeping porches. The other rooms are furnished on practically the same scale as the front room, all having beautiful rugs on the floors.

Mr. and Mrs. Sunday are proud of their Winona home, and they make no effort to conceal their pride. The Sundays there are as different from the Sundays of the tabernacle as day and night.

Sunday in the pulpit is a fiery orator; a magnetic figure who commands men; a son of thunder who utters words of fire, that are sometimes far from being conventional. In his home he is a quiet, orderly sort of person, who romps with his children, pets his dog, and makes a companion and chum of his wife.

Catching sight of Sunday moving restlessly about in front of his home, collarless, and with his coat collar turned up and pinned about his throat, one has the impression he is looking at an invalid, who is just receiving his first breath of fresh air after a long confinement indoors. He moves rapidly about among the shrubbery, paying no attention to those about him, unless he is addressed, or finds interest in the conversation.

This is the picture he presented on the lawn in front of his home that day, but the photograph taken at that time shows quite a different sort of man. Before he had his old white hat drawn down over his eyes, but in the picture the hat is gone and the face is shown.

That face is the strongest thing about his appearance.

The life of Billy Sunday, and his success as an evangelist, is written on his countenance. He has piercing eyes, which reveal his various emotions. He has an unusually plentiful stock of hair for a man fifty years old, and his chin is normal.

He and his wife walked down to the Winona traction station with their visitors, he going for the exercise and she to meet a friend coming in on the car.

Both were in a talkative mood, and had much to say of Winona; the pretty place it is in the summertime, and the difficulties encountered in cleaning it up every year for the warm weather season. When Sunday does talk, it is with much animation.

He had many of the Winona college students at work on the grounds, putting them in order. He pays them out of his own pocket, and in return for this has the pleasure of directing their work, and having things done to suit him. The most of the students he knew by their first names, and nearly all of them greeted him as " Professor."

Mrs. Sunday has been a greater traveler than her husband, in so far as mileage goes, for in almost every meeting she has had to fly like a shuttle, back and forth between the tabernacle and home. Many women claim that they have sometimes had to live for weeks in a trunk, but Mrs. Sunday has often had to do the same in a suitcase. Indeed, she almost has to keep one packed and ready to fly at a moment's notice to the place from which the hurry call comes.

When she is at home, along comes a telegram or a long distance call, saying she is badly needed at the front, and she has to put on her hat, and without waiting to see whether it is on straight or not, do some lively sprinting to make the train. And then, sometimes almost before she has had time to become rested from the long trip, the wires begin from the other end, and bring the lively news that one of the boys has broken a leg, got the short end of a wishbone fast in his throat or been almost drowned while boating on the lake, and again she must grab up her hat and put it on in the hack, as the horses gallop for the depot.

You will know what a wonderful woman she is when we tell you that these emergency calls never flurry her. She keeps her head and her wits, and goes right on in the line of duty, without ever once breaking step, with a calmness and deliberation that do honor to her Scotch heritage. Cupid certainly did a good day's work when he caused Billy to lose his heart to a lassie whose parents were born in the Highlands.

While in a meeting six years ago it was found that one of the boys would have to be operated on for appendicitis, and while the campaign was on at Wichita, Kan., Mrs. Sunday had to scorch back to the home at Winona Lake, because Willie had broken a leg. While she was helping Mr. Sunday in the campaign at Erie, Pa., she had to take a fast train, and do it quick, for Ames, Iowa, where George was in college, and take the young man to Rochester, Minn., for a surgical operation.

The children are strong and healthy, and every one of them has the energy of a dynamo, but accidents will happen, you know, and with Billy's boys no prophet can ever tell just when or how.

XVII

RESULTS OF MEETINGS IN VARIOUS PLACES

ALL things considered, the greatest meeting held by Mr. Sunday so far, was at Columbus, Ohio, in January and February of 1913. Eighteen thousand conversions were recorded, and twelve thousand of these had united with churches within two weeks of the close of the campaign. The following summing up of this meeting was given by a correspondent of the *Western Christian Advocate,* a most conservative paper:

"The Sunday meetings have closed in Columbus, Ohio, with the unanimous judgment that all previous evangelistic records, in point of number of converts, and in funds raised, have been eclipsed. The meeting continued through seven weeks, and every day the interest increased until the entire city was held in its grasp. It is said that every department of the city's activities was influenced.

"The straightening up of men's lives meant the arousing of the sense of obligation and feeling of honesty. Old debts were paid to grocerymen and other parties to such an extent that it became a matter of public notice and commendation of the spirit of the revival. If this is one of the results of Mr. Sunday's meetings, it furnishes a recommendation that will appeal to business men. There are many communities where such a meeting would be welcomed by the hard-headed business men, who are carrying on their books hundreds of dollars against families belonging to the church. One of the greatest recommendations for modern revivalism is its power to awaken men to their obligation to pay their debts.

"Every walk of life was influenced. It could not be resisted. It went into every office, every shop, every home, every street. It claimed converts in every profession. The police of the city were captured. Every policeman placed on duty at the tabernacle "hit the sawdust trail." The chief himself, seated on the platform, made a hearty and open confession of Christ. Lawyers, physicians, merchants, artisans of every description, all gave their quota to the harvest of the evangelist. One pastor writes: ' The work cannot be conservatively and sanely described. It would be like trying to describe a cyclone when you are in the midst of its fury.'

"Men and women were carried off their feet. Men who had never listened to a religious appeal, surrendered to the call of Christ. Many who had hated evangelism and feared the gospel were caught in the throes of decision. The total number of converts during the campaign was eighteen thousand one hundred and forty-nine.

"There were ninety-five tabernacle meetings held, and the aggregate attendance was nearly a million people. On the last Saturday night four thousand Free and Accepted Masons attended the meeting, led by two bands of music. This demonstration revealed one of the great powers of the evangelist. All manner of secular influences may be carried into his meetings, but they do not affect the situation. He picks up the burden, and like a Samson walks off with it. Nothing seems to be great enough to eclipse the spiritual influence. The larger the crowd the greater the results. A choir of two thousand voices and the prayers of sixty churches is a tremendous support for any preacher of the gospel.

"On the last Sabbath people were standing at the tabernacle doors before eight o'clock, with their dinner baskets on their arms, there to spend the day. At nine o'clock Mr. Sunday preached to the prisoners in the State Prison, with splendid results; fifteen hundred men responding to his appeal. The crowd at the morning service was a jam, but marvelous for spiritual uplift. In the afternoon the attendance upon the men's meeting was thirteen thousand five hundred, the greatest number of men ever present at a religious meeting at one time.

"Simultaneously with the men's meeting Mrs. Sunday addressed a mass meeting of women which numbered thousands in attendance. The evening service was one great rally of the forces and converts, which resulted for the day's work in twenty-three hundred and thirty-one conversions, aggregating eighteen thousand one hundred and forty-nine, and the raising of $20,795.62 for the expenses of the campaign.

"This is registered as the universal judgment: ' Every one was tired; every one was happy; every one was satisfied.' This further result must also be registered: The reinstatement of evangelistic methods into favor in the minds of men, and the popularizing of personal approach in matters of religion; and this final word, that faith in the response of men to the religious appeal has been greatly heightened."

The *Ohio State Journal,* a daily paper which freely and sympathetically featured the meeting, gave this judgment at the close:

"In the opinion of men who have studied the campaigns of great revivalists, this record surpasses all figures thus far compiled in the United States and abroad, and may be taken as the greatest evangelistic demonstration of modern times. For more than seven weeks hundreds of business men had neglected their private affairs; for an equal period social engagements were disregarded or side-tracked; for that length of time sixty churches had closed their doors, the pastors had devoted the most of their time to advancing the work of the campaign, and during all those days the Rev. Billy Sunday, the baseball evangelist, had talked and prayed, sweated and pranced about the platform, besought and entreated with sinners, flayed with scalding invective every sort of wickedness, and endeared himself personally to multitudes who either had been openly or covertly antagonistic. Under the spell of his oratory and the persuasive influence of his co-workers, all manner of men were made to take a new view of life. City and county officials, saloon-keepers and professors, society women and shop-girls, school children and avowed agnostics stood up and said, ' I publicly accept Jesus Christ as my personal Saviour.' "

And this from another issue of the same paper:

" Now that the Sunday meetings are over, it may be well to take an account of stock. Mr. Sunday has been given a hearing that has not been rivaled in the history of the church. It is very important that a hearing should be obtained, and it is very probable that Rev. William Sunday's peculiarities of style may have made this feature successful. At any rate twice as many people went to hear him as could gain admission to his great tabernacle.

" The advantage that Mr. Sunday took of these great throngs was to preach a religion of life and not of doctrine. He had his doctrine, but its underlying lesson was that of a pure and honest life. No man ever brought to the masses the alternative of right and wrong, of decency and disgrace, of purity and vice, as did Rev. Sunday in proclaiming his doctrine.

" As a result of his mission here, we should say there

PITTSBURG TABERNACLE. ESTIMATED SEATING CAPACITY 15,000.

is a stronger moral sense in this community than there ever was before; and now, the pressing question is, how to preserve it; how to make it vital in civic, religious and business life. He has made of religion a thoroughly practical matter, and has made the people feel it to be that way. And now it becomes the duty of every one who loves his neighbors and his city to put into practice in his own life the high lessons of duty and honor and faith which he has been preaching to us for the last seven weeks."

In 1910 Mr. Sunday held a meeting at Newcastle, Pa. Two years later the following was published by the *News* of that city, written by Rev. A. B. McCormick, a Presbyterian pastor, who frankly confesses that he had been much prejudiced against Sunday before the holding of the meeting:

"In a city of nearly forty thousand there have been only eighty-three arrests in the past two months! There is no open saloon in either city or county. And this must largely be credited to Mr. Sunday's preaching in general, and to his famous ' booze sermon ' in particular. At its close about six thousand men pledged themselves to stand against alcohol at their first opportunity.

"Our churches are in a prosperous condition. Two large buildings are in process of erection. Four churches have been enlarged. Several others have been repaired and re-decorated. Four have purchased new organs. Others have paid debts of long standing. A new hundred-thousand-dollar Y. M. C. A. building has been erected. A whirlwind campaign for fifteen hundred members for it resulted in securing sixteen hundred and twenty-five. A Rescue Mission has been established, and the people have rallied to its support. It is open every night in the week, and many remarkable conversions are reported.

A band of personal workers, most of whom were Sunday converts, have carried the message of personal evangelism to many communities, and have been blessed of God in conducting some genuine revivals. One of them has become an evangelist, and has just closed a successful campaign. The movement for Christian unity has received great impetus. The people of the various churches worship and work together in a harmony delightful to witness.

" The revival was worth while. The Lord sets his seal to Mr. Sunday's preaching. He knows but one gospel—' Jesus Christ and Him crucified.' It is still the power of God unto salvation. May God bless him, and save him for many years of evangelism."

In the winter of 1908 a Sunday meeting was held at Decatur, Ill., which beat all the records up to that time. A year later a correspondent of a Chicago paper visited Decatur, and had this to say about the results of the meeting:

" The church life of the city is unusually well established. Few places of thirty thousand can boast so many fine church buildings, and new pastors coming to the community recognize at once that the church work is remarkably well supported, and engages the energies of a very large percentage of the prominent business and professional men. On the subject the pastors were a unit. Though some voted for Mr. Sunday with great reluctance, fearing the sensationalism of his work, they all accepted the final decision heartily, and entered into the meetings with the determination to reap the largest possible return. Finally, the work of preparation was thoroughly done. The evangelist came into a field which had been thoroughly brought to the most perfect degree of ripeness, and was met by laborers with their sleeves rolled up.

" After discounting the reports of the newspapers to the limit, on the score of local pride, it must still be conceded that the Decatur meetings were notable in the history of modern evangelism. The huge tabernacle was packed afternoon and evening throughout the whole six weeks, and on Sunday afternoons, when Sunday spoke to men alone, as many as six thousand men were crowded inside.

" People flocked into the city from Bloomington, and even farther, and the local papers within a radius of twenty miles reported additions to their churches when the meetings closed. It is easily possible in a city of this size to have even so large a meeting in progress in one corner and not affect greatly the life and activity of the town, but it was not so in Decatur. The newspapers turned their pages over bodily to the report of the meeting, printing from twelve to fifteen columns a day, and making special subscription offers which added thousands of short term subscribers to their lists. There were no social engagements. Lodges did not meet, and study, both in the schools and the University, was maintained only with the greatest difficulty.

" Near the close interest in the meeting took on added zest, as it was seen that the record of Bloomington, the rival of Decatur, was to be equaled and passed. It became a matter of earnest community effort that the meetings should attain a huge success. Men closed their places of business at the evangelist's request, and came to swell the attendance figures. Even baseball gave way before the tidal wave. Sunday and sin and salvation were literally the sole topics of conversation.

" Out of this there came six thousand two hundred and nine converts, and an offering to Mr. Sunday amounting to $11,379.56, the largest amount he had ever received. The results of such a meeting are to be measured by their effect on the churches first, and then on the life and the thought of the town.   In all cases the second of these measurements is hardest to make.   But in Decatur it is its effect on the city life which is most prominent; the thing which one is compelled to recognize.   It rises up to confront you, whether you talk with the mayor or the bootblack.   It is written all over the police records and the polling booths, and he that runs may read.   I had to talk to a good many men before I was willing to admit this.   But when, after a dozen interviews, in which a dozen business men had told me the same thing, I sat in the office of one of the most prominent lawyers and politicians in the city, and heard him say, ' I do not think that any man can measure the permanent good which Mr. Sunday did this town,' I ceased objecting, and was convinced.

" I suggested to the proprietor of a gents' furnishing store that Billy Sunday is a grafter, just to see what he would do, and I had to take it all back before he would sell me a shirt.   The bootblacks said, ' He is the only man who ever came to Decatur who prayed for everybody!'   The telephone girls wanted to chip in something for Billy because ' he prayed for us.'

" The business man who is leading the largest faction of the now disorganized Republican party, said: ' If there should be a proposition to invite Sunday here again, we could form as strong a committee as we had before, and form it entirely outside of the churches.'

" So much for the sentiment of the town toward Sunday and the effect of his work on its life.   Twelve churches united in inviting him to Decatur, and stood solidly behind him through it all.   But the interesting thing is that even the churches which did not co-operate could not escape some measure of the result."

The following is from the South Bend *Tribune:*

" The greatest religious revival in Indiana is now history. For seven weeks South Bend, Mishawaka and surrounding territory have been stirred as never before. Six thousand three hundred and ninety-eight persons have taken Billy Sunday by the hand, thereby signifying their intention of living new lives. How many others of the five hundred and sixty-six thousand who attended the meetings have inwardly made the same resolve, no one can say. Nor can any say how many professing Christians have been uplifted by the meetings.

" If there is one thing that keeps alive religious life and religious institutions, it is the evangelistic spirit. The permanent organization of a ' personal workers' league ' among men is a prophecy of greater and more effective church work in South Bend and Mishawaka than ever before. These men have joined themselves and pledged their services in assisting the pastors in keeping alive the evangelistic fires. If they persist in their purpose the churches will not become ' religious ice boxes,' as Mr. Sunday calls them.

" The revival has meant much to South Bend and Mishawaka in an economic sense. Saloon men themselves estimate their business in the two cities has fallen off forty per cent. It is stated on good authority, that last week, notwithstanding the hot weather, ten thousand more pounds of meat were brought to South Bend than usual. If figures could be obtained the same showing would undoubtedly be made for Mishawaka. Merchants have been surprised to see old, outlawed accounts paid up, and ' conscience money ' has been paid for stolen articles. One merchant as far away as Elwood, Ind., felt the results of the meetings when he received two dollars for a knife stolen years ago. Family quarrels have been adjusted; family friendships have been cemented; family altars erected. These are evidences of quickened individual consciences, and quickened individual consciences will surely mean quickened social consciences, which mean more attention paid to matters of government, and better enforcement of law.

"The religious revival has done much for South Bend, Mishawaka and the surrounding territory in a religious and economic way, but its beneficence does not stop there. The spirit of giving has been spread abroad. Hundreds of persons who never before contributed to any cause, have had a part in bearing the expense of the meeting. That very fact has encouraged the development of a spirit of municipal solidarity. Local pride has been captured in the fields where it was running wild, utterly useless, and has been harnessed and put to work. South Bend and Mishawaka have pulled together as they never have before, with the result that there has come about a better understanding and a better feeling. It has shown that team work pays. Because these cities have seen fit to 'desire earnestly the better things,' many others have been added unto them also."

The *Record* of Wilkes-Barre, Pa., sums up results there in this way:

"A review of the seven weeks of evangelistic campaign is a mighty tribute to the extraordinary genius and talent of Mr. Sunday. The number of those who have professed Christianity runs away up into the thousands, and the results in the abstract are simply beyond comprehension. More thousands than those who have 'hit the trail' will lead better lives. Their hearts have been touched. Many of them will be led to join the throng of active Christians after the Sunday party has left the city.

"At the beginning of the campaign the people went out of curiosity. They wanted to see and hear the man about whom so much had been said. Skepticism prevailed. Sneers were heard on every hand. It was deemed impossible that a baseball player who had drifted into the ministry could move the self-complacent, intelligent element in the Wyoming Valley into such a spirit of religious enthusiasm as was reported from other places. It seemed entirely out of the question. The story of to-day is the story of a wonderful revelation. The baseball evangelist has accomplished the seemingly impossible. The community has been stirred from center to circumference. Skepticism has given way to conviction, and conviction has been followed by enthusiasm.

"The work of Mr. Sunday is on the lips of tens of thousands of the people. Already thousands of applications for church membership have been made, and other thousands will follow. Hundreds of men who squandered their earnings and their health in drunkenness have been torn loose from the old habits. Hundreds of men whose brutality in the midst of their families was a constant heartbreak to distressed wives and terror-stricken children, have for the first time shed the sunshine of cheer into their homes. Tens of thousands will gird on the armor of civic righteousness, and move forward to do battle with the forces of evil. The Wyoming Valley will be a better place to live in.

"A man who can accomplish such results is not an ordinary man. His methods may be unique, and he may have been advertised as no other evangelist has been advertised; yet over and above it all is the fact that if he had not spoken the plain truth in a way to carry conviction into the hearts of the skeptics and the luke-warm, the actual results of his campaign in spiritual and moral cleansing would not have been so tremendous, so astounding. Say what you will—here are the results.

" At the conclusion of these seven weeks of Billy Sunday, there is no uncertain answer to the question propounded at the outset: ' Will he make good?' The affirmative answer comes in a mighty chorus from every part of the Valley; from homes made happier; from men and women reclaimed and re-consecrated, and from tens of thousands who have felt the touch of a new inspiration: Mr. Sunday has made good."

The following was written by C. W. Laycock, a business man of Wilkes-Barre, some months after the close of the campaign there:

" The religious impressions made here by the Billy Sunday campaign are so deep and the work of grace so far-reaching that one is bewildered by the magnitude of the wonders God has wrought. Sunday himself is a wonder, but after recognizing all his natural endowments, and allowing for the quickening of his faculties through devotion and consecration to a great cause, there is something more to be accounted for, an influence which pervades the whole community for miles around.

" To illustrate : Twelve miles out in the country a farm-hand who had not been to hear Mr. Sunday preach, nor had he read any of his sermons, heard that there was a great revival here and many people were being converted. He was impressed with the thought that something more was needed in his own life, so he went to a friend and told him that he wanted to know how he could find Jesus Christ and be saved. The friend advised him to read the book of Acts. This he knew nothing about, and was informed that it was in the Bible. He walked a mile and borrowed a Bible from a neighbor, which he took home and read and studied until his interest was greatly intensified; yet he was not satisfied. So he went to the man for whom he worked and said he must go to Wilkes-Barre.

"When asked how long he would be gone he said, 'I don't know. I have a big job on hand, and don't know how long it is going to take.' He put in his grip enough food to last a week and went to the railroad station, but reached it too late for the train. Rather than wait another day he walked twelve miles, but did not reach here until after the close of the afternoon meeting at the tabernacle. He finally found his way to a parsonage, and when asked by the minister what he wanted, said: "I want somebody to tell me how to find Christ."

"The minister told him he had gotten to about the right place, and after some conversation and prayer the man arose, his face aglow, and said: 'Well, if I had known this I wouldn't have brought so many victuals with me.' He then went home entirely satisfied. That man is now an active member of the church of his choice, and is teaching a Bible class. I mention this incident merely to show that God so honors Mr. Sunday with the presence of His Spirit that when the people fully co-operate with him, there is manifested an influence which is wonderful in its workings.

"Prior to the Sunday campaign one of the Young Men's Christian Associations in our valley had an average attendance of twelve to fifteen at its Sunday afternoon meetings. Interest there has grown until last Sunday there were seven hundred and fifty at the afternoon meeting, and what is also interesting is that many of these meetings are being led by men who were converted in the Sunday meetings.

"As far as I can learn there is no abatement of religious interest and zeal among those who were converted, and many who did not take their stand on the side of Christianity are still talking about the wonderful things that have come to pass.

"Business men tell me they have received 'conscience money' in amounts ranging from forty cents to twenty-five dollars. In some instances the people brought it themselves, and made open confession of their misdoings. One woman returned forty cents for goods she had stolen fifteen years ago. A man who is a clerk in a large store went to a former employer, and confessed to having stolen five dollars and thirty-five cents ten years ago. He said Billy Sunday told him he could not be a thief and a Christian at the same time, and after praying and crying the whole night through he had come to make good.

"Another instance is that of a man consulting a lawyer, stating that he expected to be sued for a bill, and to the lawyer's mind made a pretty good defense, but as suit had not been entered, and no papers served, the lawyer told him to wait until such service was made, and then come to him and he would prepare the case. About a week later the man appeared, and when the lawyer asked him to restate his defense the man simply said:

"'There is no defense; the debt is an honest one and should be paid.'

"The lawyer reminded him of the defense he seemed to have made a week earlier, when he was informed by the man that he 'had hit the trail' and was going to pay the debt.

"Enough concrete examples of changed lives and

habits can be found in this community to fill a large volume, and would make most interesting reading.

" One line of business adversely affected is the liquor business. Reliable people have told me that the business of the saloon-keepers has fallen off from thirty to seventy-five per cent.

" Cab-drivers say that the gambling and red-light district has had much less patronage. Two gambling dens and four houses have closed, and some of the 'population' have left town.

" The religious and moral atmosphere of the community is greatly improved and intensified. People marvel at the wonderful changes that have taken place, and are still occurring.

" Another result of the campaign is the more friendly feeling which now exists among the various religious denominations, a willingness to meet on common ground for a common cause."

XVIII

SUNDAY'S ORDINATION AND VARIOUS
OTHER MATTERS

IN 1905 Mr. Sunday was ordained a minister in the
Presbyterian Church, by the Chicago Presbytery,
the ordination taking place at the Jefferson Park
Presbyterian Church, in which he had for several years
been an elder. His old friend and associate in evangelistic work, Dr. J. Wilbur Chapman, preached the sermon,
and Dr. Alexander Patterson gave the charge.

In his examination before the Presbytery, the former
ball player was plied with questions for an hour or more
by the professors of theology and the learned members
of the body. He answered their questions to their entire
satisfaction, and his orthodoxy was pronounced sound in
every particular.

Occasionally some erudite professor would ask him a
question that was a poser, to which he would immediately
reply: "That's too deep for me," or "I will have to pass
that up."

He created an excellent impression by his frank, honest
manner, and the rapidity with which he gave his answers.

On June 13, 1912, the degree of Doctor of Divinity
was conferred upon Mr. Sunday by Westminster College,
at New Wilmington, Pa. In regard to this, Dr. R. M.
Russell, the President of Westminster, has well said:

"We count it to the honor of Westminster that she
did this thing. Mr. Sunday knows his Bible, which is

the true body of Divinity in theological lore. He has
devoted his life to the supreme task of world evangeliza-
tion, for which the Bible is the great charter. He is,
therefore, both in scholarship and practical effort, entitled
to the degree.

"Just as a doctor of medicine is supposed to know
the science of medicine, and practice the art of healing,
so a Doctor of Divinity who knows the truth about God,
and practices the art of saving, is entitled to the degree.
In many institutions it is customary to bestow the hon-
orary degree of Doctor of Divinity upon those who are
men more noted for their knowledge of ' the traditions
of the scribes and Pharisees ' than for their knowledge
and practical use of the Bible itself."

After being twenty-four years in the cornerstone of the
old Central Y. M. C. A. building, at Cleveland, Ohio, a
copper box containing interesting enclosures was recently
removed. Among the contents of the box was a copy
of " Cleveland's Young Men," a Y. M. C. A. publication
printed in 1889, which contained an account of the preaching, in the Star Theater, of " a deserving young ball
player named William A. Sunday." How little the writer
of those long-buried lines dreamed that the " deserving
young ball player " would one day have the whole country
at his feet.

In Sunday's meeting at Steubenville, Ohio, some time
ago, a former saloon-keeper arose and gave this remarkable testimony:

" It would take a lifetime for me to tell of the goodness
of God, and the benefit Billy Sunday did me. I kept
a saloon two miles away from the tabernacle in Columbus, but read the papers, and through them I was converted."

When this man sat down another arose and said:

" I didn't own a saloon, but was trying to buy them all—drinking, gambling and carousing around. Sunday brought me the message that brought me to Christ."

A little later on Dr. Day, pastor of the First Presbyterian Church, of Columbus, and President of the Ohio State Society of Christian Endeavor, said:

" I don't believe there was a man more hated in Columbus on the 27th day of last December than Billy Sunday, and a few weeks later when he left, I don't think there was a person more generally beloved, honored and respected than this man of God. I staked one of the men who gave testimony here this evening to two hundred dollars to start a restaurant. He has paid me back that money a long time ago, and has an account in the bank besides. It would take me a long time to tell you of the good that has been done. On the last day of the meeting in Columbus two thousand confessed their faith in Christ, and there were scarcely any children among them. If there has ever been anything like that since Pentecost it has not been recorded. Nine thousand united with churches within two weeks after the close of Sunday's meeting, and from the close until June 1 the accessions to our churches totaled twelve thousand."

Walter Holliday, of Columbus, Ohio, is an agent for the Standard Oil Company in China. While the Sunday meetings were in progress in his home city, the papers containing accounts of them and reports of the sermons, were sent to him by his sister, and these led to his awakening and conversion, thirteen thousand miles away from the tabernacle. He wrote at once to the pastor of his sister's church, asking to be enrolled as a member of the same. Here is something for the people who do not think that God is using Billy Sunday to think about.

While Sunday was holding a meeting at Erie, Pa.,

eighteen hundred dollars were given in the basket collections in a single day. If this has ever been equaled in any religious meeting, history has failed to mention it.

On the third Sunday of the Steubenville, Ohio, campaign, the basket collections for the day were $1,548.90.

The first convert in the meeting at Pontiac, Ill., was a young woman, who inaugurated a movement that resulted in the building of a fine Y. M. C. A. building.

At the Men's Meeting on the last day of the Columbus campaign, six hundred and nine men " hit the trail " and broke the record which had been held by McKeesport, and which was later outdone by Wilkes-Barre, on the last day in the great campaign in that city, when six hundred and eleven men were enrolled at the afternoon meeting for men. It is impossible to appreciate the immensity or intensity of these great men's meetings, in which hundreds of men are won for Christ in a single meeting, and many of them influential men in the city and state. It is marvelous.

When the invitation was given one night in the Steubenville meeting, the mayor of the city was the first to go forward.

Sunday has a golden text that has become a great tower and bulwark in his daily life and work, and it is this:

> " Study to show thyself approved unto God, a workman that needeth not to be ashamed, rightly dividing the word of truth."—2 Tim. 2:15.

It is doubtful if there are many hours in the day when this great text does not come into his mind. It has become almost a part of his signature, for seldom or never does he sign a check without following his name with the reference, as below:

W. A Sunday
V. Sim. 2: 15.

Those who are closely associated with him and know him well, are confident that he earnestly strives to fashion his life and his preaching according to the manner indicated by his golden text. It is this that makes him so utterly fearless in the pulpit. It is this that makes him dare to preach in his own way, no matter who may criticise. It is this that makes him as conscientious in what he preaches and how he preaches as he is in paying his debts.

Sunday has no fear of man, because whenever he preaches he believes that he is standing in the one spot in all the universe where the Lord of hosts wants him to be at that very moment. What matter, then, who may howl and growl and throw mud at him? And he is just as confident that the sermon he is about to preach will be a message direct from the Almighty, and he has no more fear of its falling dead like a flash in the pan, than he has of missing his dinner. He goes to the pulpit " studying to show himself approved unto God (in the work he will do there), as a workman that needeth not to be ashamed," and he intends to rightly divide the word of truth, according to the light that has been given him, no matter who may be wounded, healed or offended by it.

It may be that one reason why the ministry of some preachers appears to be as fruitless as the barren fig tree, is that they never expect the Lord to be within ten miles of the pulpit in which they do their preaching, but nothing like that is ever true of Sunday. He always counts upon the Lord being in the meeting, no matter who else may stay away. He believes the Lord will stand by him, no matter what the conditions or the weather may be. If he didn't feel absolutely sure of this he would never hold another meeting.

When he undertakes a new meeting there is no uncertainty in his mind about what the result will be. He is as sure that thousands will be converted as he is that the sun will shine to-morrow. Failure is never even taken into consideration. In Sunday's dictionary there is no such word as fail. He pulled that word out by the roots long ago, and has grown a faith that keeps it out. His preaching has been criticised with more venom than that of any other preacher of the present day, but not a whisper of insinuation has ever been turned against his faith. He has a faith that gives more than one big mountain marching orders wherever he goes, and no one knows it better than the man who has never been able to speak to a molehill in a way to even shake it.

Sunday is the man he is to-day, and preaches as he does, and preaches what he does, mainly because he believes the Bible from cover to cover. It is doubtful if such a thing as a doubt ever troubles him, for he seems to have utterly destroyed Amalek, root and branch. He has no more doubt that the Bible is the word of God, than he doubts that the letters he receives from his wife have been written by her hand. When he reads the Bible —and he spends much time over its golden pages—it is that he may learn the will of " Him whom having not seen " he loves, and when he learns what that will is, it becomes his prayer that it may be done in, by and through him. To make his preaching as effective as it should be, he knows that he must live just as high as he preaches, and every sermon he preaches to the multitudes that flock to hear him, he first preaches just as prayerfully to himself.

Could Sunday once be robbed of the comfort, peace and rest he derives from his golden text, and the almost hourly consolation and inspiration he finds flowing out of it, like water from the smitten rock, he would no doubt soon be shorn of his strength. In his constant use of his golden text there seems to be repeated in him the experience of the wrestler in the fable, who was at once made fresh and strong again every time he touched the earth.

Here is a partial list of the many towns and cities in which Sunday has held meetings:

IOWA

Audubon
Afton
Atlantic
Alta
Avoca
Bedford
Boone
Burlington
Cedar Rapids
Centerville
Clarksburg
Colesburg
Corydon
Cumberland
Davenport
Des Moines
Dubuque
Dunlap
Eddyville
Elliott
Emerson
Exira
Fairfield
Fonda
Fredericksburg
Garner
Glenwood
Glidden
Gravity
Grundy Center
Harlan
Hawkeye
Iowa Falls
Jefferson
Keokuk
Knoxville
Leon
Malvern
Marshalltown
Mason City
Muscatine
Nevada
New Hampton
New Sharon
Osceola
Oelwein
Oakville
Olin
Ottumwa
Panora
Perry
Seymour
Sibley
Sigourney
Silver City
Sioux City
Strawberry Point
Stuart
Tabor
Villisca
Wapella
Waterloo
Williamsburg

ILLINOIS

Aledo
Belvidere
Bloomington
Canton
Carthage
Charleston
Chicago
Danville
Decatur
Dixon
Dundee
Elgin
Farmington
Freeport
Galesburg
Galva
Genoa
Gibson City
Harvard
Harvey
Jacksonville
Kankakee
Kewanee
Macomb
Marengo
Murphysboro
Oneida
Princeton
Pontiac
Prophetstown
Rantoul
Richmond
Rockford
Savanna
Springfield
Sterling
West Pullman
Wheaton
Woodstock

OHIO

Canton
Cincinnati
Columbus
Dayton
East Liverpool
Lima

Portsmouth
Springfield
Steubenville
Toledo
Youngstown

NEBRASKA
Beatrice
Humbodlt
Lincoln
Oklahoma City
Omaha
Oxford
Pawnee City
Tecumseh

PENNSYLVANIA
Beaver Falls
Erie
Johnstown
McKeesport
Newcastle
Philadelphia,
Pittsburg
Scranton
Sharon
Wilkes-Barre

WASHINGTON
Bellingham
Everett
Spokane

INDIANA
Fairmount
Hammond
Richmond
Salem
South Bend

MINNESOTA
Austin
Browns Valley
Buffalo
Duluth
Ely
Marshall
Moorehead
Redwood
Rochester
Tower
Wilmar
Worthington

MISSOURI
Joplin
Kansas City
Marysville

FLORIDA
Daytona
Jacksonville
St. Augustine
Tampa

COLORADO
Boulder
Cañon City
Denver
Salida

NEW YORK
Buffalo
New York City
Syracuse

VIRGINIA
Moline
Norfolk
Norton
Richmond
Roanoke
Rock Island

TENNESSEE
Bristol
Chattanooga
Knoxville
Morristown

W. VIRGINIA
Beckley
Bluefield
Charleston
Fairmont
Huntington
Logan

Lynchburg
Wheeling

S. CAROLINA
Columbia
Spartansburg

MICHIGAN
Detroit
Ludington
Manistee
Atlanta, Ga.
Baltimore, Md.
Belleville, Wis.
Boston, Mass.
Colorado Sprgs,
  Colo.
Fargo, N. D.
Fort Worth,
  Tex.
Los Angeles,
  Cal.
Louisville, Ky.
Providence, R.I.
Sisseton,
  So. Dak.
Trenton, N. J.
Tulsa, Okla.
Washington,
  D. C.
Wichita, Kan.

There are two hundred and three names in the list given above. To say that Sunday has spoken to an average of fifteen thousand different persons for each meeting, would be a very low estimate, and yet it would make the total number to which he has preached, two million one hundred and thirty thousand, and probably half as many more have read printed reports of his sermons. It is not likely that any other man ever preached to so many people.

To say that there have been an average of four thousand converts enrolled for each meeting held, would also be putting it low, but at that figure the grand total would be five hundred and sixty-eight thousand! And yet there are people—and some of them are preachers—who do not believe that God is using Billy Sunday.

XIX

A HARD HITTER OF THE LIQUOR TRAFFIC

IT is doubtful if any man in modern times has done
more than Billy Sunday to help the cause of temperance. At all events, this is the inference from
the vigorous way in which the whisky interests oppose
him. The liquor men seem to know his engagements
almost as soon as he makes them, and weeks ahead of
his meetings they begin to circulate all manner of lying
slanders against him. It is well authenticated that
they spend thousands of dollars every year in doing
this.

His great " booze sermon " is one of the most effective
and hard-hitting specimens of eloquence against the
saloon that ever fell from the lips of man. If every man
in the country could hear him hurl it forth, as Jove
hurled thunderbolts, it would hasten the coming of the
glad day when the whisky dragon shall be forever destroyed.

Sunday has done effective work for the cause of temperance, not only in his own revival campaigns, but on
special occasions between meetings. In his campaigns
he always observes Monday as a rest day, but it is
seldom a day of rest for him. He is so besieged with
calls from other towns and cities to pay them a visit that
almost every Monday he is speaking at some other point,
fifty or a hundred, or even two hundred miles away from
the place of his own meeting, and in such addresses he

generally gives the whisky business some telling sledge-hammer blows.

Many times temperance interests have chartered a special Pullman car, into which they have loaded Sunday and several of his party, and sent them out to cover as much territory as could be reached in this way in the few days intervening between meetings. This was done in the state of Illinois with such success that hundreds of saloons were closed, and many counties went dry.

Beginning with the first of January, 1908, Sunday conducted a five weeks' campaign in Bloomington, Ill., a city of twenty-seven thousand in the central part of the state. This meeting resulted in forty-seven hundred people taking their stand for God and righteousness. After a few days' intermission he entered upon another campaign at Decatur, a city of thirty-four thousand, forty miles south of Bloomington, and this meeting resulted in six thousand two hundred and nine conversions. The next meeting was at Charleston, about seventy-five miles southeast of Decatur.

The Illinois spring election came on a Tuesday in the midst of this last campaign. For many days previous Sunday had been going out to different towns and cities over the state, giving his "booze sermon" and then rushing back to Charleston for the evening meeting.

When the spring elections were over it was found that fifteen hundred saloons had been knocked out in one day, and much of this was directly the result of Sunday's efforts. In Decatur sixty-three saloons were closed, and in Charleston twenty-one were put out of business.

A goodly number of other towns and cities that had been considered hopelessly wet, were listed in the dry column. And so it is safe to say that many of the hardest blows the saloon giant has ever received have been dealt it by Billy Sunday.

On the eve of the great campaign for state wide prohibition in West Virginia, Sunday covered the state in a special train, speaking at several places every day, and there is no doubt whatever but that his strenuous labors in that campaign turned the tide that brought in the great wave of an overwhelming majority for the cause of God and public decency.

It is quite fitting, in this connection, to quote a few statements from the " booze sermon," to show how unflinchingly and courageously Sunday deals sledgehammer blows full in the face of the liquor traffic:

" The saloon is the sum of all villainies. It is worse than war or pestilence. It is the crime of crimes. It is the parent of crimes, and the mother of sins. It is the appalling source of misery, poverty and sorrow. It causes three-fourths of the crime, and of course is the source of three-fourths of the taxes to support that crime. And to license such an incarnate fiend of hell is the dirtiest, most low down, damnable business on top of this old earth.

" The saloons fill the jails and the penitentiaries, the poorhouses and insane asylums. Who has to pay the bills? The landlord who doesn't get the rent, because the money goes for whisky, the butcher and the grocer and the charitable person who takes pity on the children of drunkards, and the taxpayer who supports the insane asylums and other institutions, that the whisky business fills with human wrecks.

" Do away with the accursed business and you will not have to put up to support them. Who gets the money? The saloon keepers and the brewers and the distillers, while the whisky fills the land with misery, poverty, wretchedness, disease, death and damnation, and it is being authorized by the will of the sovereign people.

"You say, 'People will drink it anyway.' Not by my vote. You say, 'Men will murder their wives anyway.' Not by my vote. 'They will steal anyway.' Not by my vote. You are the sovereign people, and what are *you* going to do about it?

"Let me assemble before your minds the bodies of the drunken dead, who crawl away 'into the jaws of death, into the mouth of hell,' and then out of the valley of the shadow of the drink let me call the contingent widowhood, and wifehood and childhood, and let their tears rain down upon their purple faces! Do you think that would stop the curse of the liquor traffic? No! No!

"In these days when the question of saloon or no saloon is at the fore in almost every community, one hears a good deal about what is called 'personal liberty.' These are fine large mouth-filling words, and they certainly do sound first-rate; but when you get right down and analyze them in the light of good old horse sense, you will discover that in their application to the present controversy they mean just about this:

"Personal liberty is for the man who, if he has the inclination and the price, can stand up to a bar and fill his hide so full of red liquor that he is transformed for the time into an irresponsible, dangerous, evil-smelling brute. But personal liberty is not for the patient, long-suffering wife, who has to endure with what fortitude she may his blows and curses. Nor is it for his children, who if they escape his insane rage, are yet robbed of every known joy and privilege of childhood, and too often grow up neglected, uncared for and vicious as the result of their surroundings and the example before them.

" ' Personal liberty ' is not for the sober industrious citizen who, from the proceeds of honest toil and orderly living, has to pay, willingly or not, the tax bills which pile up as the direct result of drunkenness, disorder and poverty, the items of which are written in the records of every police court and poorhouse in the land. Nor is ' personal liberty ' for the good woman who goes abroad in the town only at the risk of being shot down by some drink-crazed demon. This rant about ' personal liberty,' as an argument, has no leg to stand upon.

" I tell you, men, the American home is the dearest heritage of the people, for the people, and by the people, and when a man can go from home in the morning with the kisses of wife and children on his lips, and come back at night with an empty dinner bucket to a happy home, that man is a better man, whether white or black. Whatever takes away the comforts of home—whatever degrades the man or woman—whatever invades the sanctity of the home, is the deadliest foe to the home, to church, to state and school, and because of what it is and does the saloon is the deadliest foe to the home, to church and school and state on top of God Almighty's dirt!

" And if all the combined forces of hell should assemble in conclave, and with them all the men on earth that hate and despise God, purity and virtue; if all the scum of the earth could mingle with the denizens of hell to try to think of the deadliest institution to home, church and state, I tell you, sir, the combined hellish intelligence could not conceive of or bring forth an institution that could touch the hem of the garment of the open licensed saloon to damn the home and manhood and womanhood and business, and every other good thing on God's earth.

"In the island of Jamaica the rats increased so they destroyed the crops, and they introduced the mongoose, which is a species of the coon. They have three breeding seasons a year, and there are twelve to fifteen in each brood, and they are deadly enemies of the rats. The result was that the rats disappeared, and there was nothing more for the mongoose to feed upon, so it attacked the snakes and the frogs and the lizards that fed upon the insects, with the result that the insects increased, and they stripped the gardens, eating up the onions and the lettuce and everything that grew in them. And then the mongoose attacked the sheep and the cats and the puppies and the calves and the geese. Now Jamaica is spending hundreds of thousands of dollars, trying to get rid of the mongoose.

"The American mongoose is the open licensed saloon. It eats the carpet off the floor, and the clothes from off your back; your money out of the bank, and it eats up character. And it goes on until it leaves a stranded wreck in the home, a skeleton of what was once brightness and happiness, and yet some of you keep right on voting, year after year, for the devilish thing to stay and go on with its deadly work of havoc and ruin.

"It is the saloon that cocks the highwayman's pistol. The saloon that puts the rope in the hands of the mob. It is the anarchist of the world, and its dirty red flag is dyed with the blood of women and children. It sent the bullet through the body of Lincoln. It nerved the arm of the assassins who struck down Garfield and McKinley.

"Yes, it is a murderer. Every plot that was ever hatched against our flag, and every anarchist plot against the government and law, was born and bred, and crawled out of the grogshop to damn this country. The curse of God Almighty is on the saloon. Legislatures are legislating against it. Decent society is barring it out. The fraternal brotherhoods are knocking it out. The secret societies are closing their doors against the whisky seller. They don't want him wriggling his carcass in their lodges. Yes, sir! I tell you the curse of God is on it. It is on the down grade. It is headed for hell, and by the grace of God I am going to give it a push, with a whoop, for all I know how. How many of you will help me?

"You men now have a chance to show your manhood. Then in the name of your pure mother, in the name of your manhood, in the name of your wife, and the pure innocent children that climb up in your lap and put their arms around your neck, in the name of all that is good and noble, fight the curse. Shall you men who hold in your hands the ballot, and in that ballot hold the destiny of womanhood and childhood and manhood, shall you, the sovereign power, refuse to rally in the name of defenseless men and women and native land? No!"

XX

SUNDAY'S VERSATILITY—ROYAL RECEPTION AT COLUMBUS

NO one who has heard Sunday through a meeting can doubt but that he would have made a fine actor, had his talents been exercised to their fullest in that direction. He impersonates almost every character he introduces, and does it well. Tom Keene, the actor, was his warm personal friend, and once urged him to become his "understudy." He had no doubt, he said, that Sunday might become one of the world's great actors.

William Jennings Bryan, another good friend of the evangelist, has said that Sunday would make one of the greatest political speakers the country has known, were he to give his attention to politics as earnestly as he has done to preaching. In one address he will astonish and delight by his dramatic portrayal and brilliant word pictures, and in the next he may excel in humor. No one can hear him for just a time or two and have anything like a clear idea of his remarkable versatility.

One newspaper writer said that "when he gave his vivid impersonation of the call of the Almighty to the great Welsh evangelist, Evan Roberts, the hearts of many stood still, and they fancied for a moment that they heard in truth the call of God to the grimy Welsh miner who came out of the coal mines in the bowels of the earth to stir his native country with a power that had

215

never been excelled, even in that spiritual and ardently religious country of bards and druids."

The *Toledo Blade* had this to say of Sunday during the great meeting he held in that city:

"He is as dramatic as the greatest actor. His story of the pearl at the end of the evening sermon was one of the most dramatic any one in Toledo has ever seen or heard. The people listened to a very simple story with eyes and mouths agape. A half-drunken and ragged man in one of the front seats who had fallen asleep, suddenly awoke at the beginning of the story, and leaned farther and farther forward during the recital, following with his body the movements of the body of the speaker, until it seemed at times that he would certainly fall from his seat. When the story ended he leaned back in his seat with a deep sigh, at the discomfiture of the man of whom the story was told.

"Sunday's good humor was also infectious, and communicated itself to the audience. Whenever he laughed the multitude laughed with him. Every point he made went home, and even those he lashed applauded the witticism with which it was clinched. Those who had come merely to have the opportunity to get at first hand some of his so-called vulgarity left disappointed, for he 'made good' with his usual language. He so deftly put the lance of criticism into the festering spots of wrong living that his words of ridicule were double-edged. They carried with them the anæsthetic of a spontaneous bubbling humor that took the pain from the wound he made.

"His mannerisms are Sundayisms. He is a master of invective and excoriating adjective, and resembles no other public speaker alive. His speech is as lightning-like and keen as are his movements. He darts about the platform with the rapidity of a hawk, and he bends and handles his lithe body with the ease that made him one of the fastest men on bases when he played baseball.

"There is not a forced or studied movement about him. Every action is telling in its force. When he sits upon his chair on the edge of the platform, every ear is bent forward a little closer to hear the story that is coming, and when he mounts his chair to thunder forth some defiance of evil, with his hands to his lips in trumpet shape, every one grows tense in anticipation of the stirring words which are to come. His climaxes are all unique and startling. No finer denunciation or challenge was ever uttered than that which ended his morning sermon, when, mounted upon his chair, he shrilled out upon the clear morning air the words: 'Come on, ye cohorts of the devil, come on, ye forces of evil, I defy you!'"

Sunday also has an imagination which at times seems almost magical, and with it he has the ability to draw striking and telling illustrations from the commonplace and everyday affairs of life that would make him a rare writer of fiction, had he only been trained to use the pen as well as he does his voice. The little incidents that he often tells of his own family life have a power that tugs at the heartstrings, and he never fails to draw illustrations from the crowds which surround him.

New thoughts seem to fill his mind every time he faces an audience, and he utters them with such pungency and apt turn of expression that they force their way into the quick comprehension and recognition of even the slowest witted who hear them. As he often says, with the taking smile for which he is noted from ocean to ocean, "I like to put the cookies on the lower shelf."

The description he gives of his first sermon is an amusing example of the manner in which he draws upon his own experience to interest and hold attention:

"When I first began to preach I diagnosed the difficulties and sins of the people as existing in the gray matter. I figured that they were all from Missouri, and that I had to show them. You ought to have heard the sermon that I got up. My, but it was a hummer! I had stacks of encyclopedias scattered around me, and all the reference books I could lay my hands on. There were words in that sermon that would have made the jaws of a Greek professor squeak for a week. When I sprung it on the poor people it went off like a firecracker that had busted in the middle.

"I figured that the Lord had got it doped out all wrong, and that I was going to hand the goods to the sinful old world that would bring it right down on its knees. I went after the devils of this thing and the devils of that thing, and yet nothing happened. Then I loaded my old muzzle-loading gospel gun with ipecac, buttermilk, rough on rats, rock salt and whatever else came handy, and the gang has been ducking and the feathers flying ever since. But I was wrong; it was the heart, and not the gray matter that was wrong. I didn't hit the ball at all until I found that out.

"I've been a preacher a good many years now, and I like it. I love it as I love nothing else. I wouldn't leave it for any money, and while I am about it, I believe in preaching so that people can understand me. Paul said he would rather speak five words that were understood than ten thousand in an unknown tongue, and that hits me. I want people to know what I mean, and that is why I try to get down to where they live. What do I care if some juff-eyed dainty little dibbly-dibbly goes tibbly-tibbly around because I use plain Anglo-Saxon words?

"And I believe the Bible is the word of God, from cover to cover, and I believe that the man who magnifies the word of God in his preaching is a man that God will honor. Why do such names stand out on the pages of history as Wesley, Whitefield, Finney and Martin Luther? Because of their fearless denunciation of all sin, and because they preached Jesus Christ without fear or favor.

"But somebody says a revival is abnormal. You lie! Do you mean to tell me that the godless card-playing conditions of the church are normal? I say they are not, but it is the abnormal state. It is the sin-sated apathetic condition in the church that is abnormal. It is the Dutch lunch and beer parties, and the card parties and the like that are abnormal. I say that they lie when they say that the revival is an abnormal condition in the church. I like these good old plain, undeniable, unmistakable words like ' lie.' It was meant for some people. It's plain; you catch the meaning when it is thrown out at some person or class of persons.

"Somebody else says, ' A revival is followed by a reaction.' I say it isn't true, but even if it were, it would be worth all it costs, because a revival brings hundreds nearer to God than they've ever been before. If your baby were sick, and you called a physician, and it grew convalescent, and you were able to keep it near you for six months more, wouldn't you think it worth while? If I can get a poor miserable sinner to turn to the Lord for six months; if I can get some maudering drunkard to go home and stop being untrue to his wife, and stop her tears for six months, by the Eternal God I'll do it every time.

"But you say, 'A revival creates undue excitement!' I take issue with you right there. It rains. The rain does the ground good. For that reason, do you want it to rain all the time? In business, is a revival unwise? You have commercial and booster clubs. Somebody says it brings disrespect upon the cause of Christianity to have a revival, because it confesses that we have back-sliders. Well, you haven't given the world any information that I don't possess, when you've said it.

"'But a revival is temporary,' some one shouts. So is a rain storm; so was Pentecost, but we are feeling the effects of it yet. We want men full of good red blood, instead of pink tea and ice water.

"You say, 'It exalts the evangelist.' Nothing of the kind. Some of you, just to find fault, say that a revival and a visiting evangelist make a bellboy of the local preacher. Well, it does not. This is not your pastor's work. He still does his. He has more opportunities under these conditions to do good. If I do not make you think more of your pastor and of his efforts, and if I don't cause you to take more interest in his efforts, I will have failed in my purpose.

"This is a day of specialists. It is a rare thing now-adays to find a general medical practitioner outside of the smaller communities. There are eye specialists, ear specialists, nose specialists and throat specialists. Some men are successes as preachers, others as pastors, and others as evangelists. I couldn't be a pastor, and many a pastor cannot be an evangelist.

"What we need is the good old-time kind of revival that will cause you to love your neighbors, and quit talking about them. A revival that will make you pay your debts and have family prayers. Get that kind, and then you will see that a revival means a very different condition from what you have imagined. Christianity means a lot more than church membership. Many an old skinflint is not fit for the balm of Gilead until you give him a fly blister and get after him with a currycomb. There are too many Sunday school teachers who are godless, card-playing, beer, wine and champagne drinkers. No wonder the kids are going to the devil. No wonder your children grow up like cattle, when you have no form of prayer in your home.

"If I knew that the chief of devils sat out there on one of those benches, and that all the cohorts of hell were in front of me, sneering and leering, I would preach anyway, and I would preach the truth as God has given it to me. It was said that when men left a meeting led by Phillips Brooks, they were filled with a desire to be preachers. I do hope that some preachers and workers for the Lord will be the fruit of these meetings."

Some idea of the great hold Sunday has on every community in which he has held a meeting may be gained from the following account of the whole-hearted welcome they gave him at Columbus, Ohio, in May, 1913, when he returned to that city for a single day, to speak at the annual Chamber of Commerce May Day Picnic. He was at the time engaged in a meeting at South Bend, Ind., but the Chamber of Commerce finally prevailed on him for once to depart from the practice he had maintained for seventeen years, of not leaving his own meeting. In order to do this a special fast train was chartered to take him from South Bend to Columbus, and return him.

The *Ohio State Journal* gave the following account of his reception and stay in Columbus:

"Turning a May day outing, in which upward of sixty-five thousand persons were interested, into a temporary tour of progress, Rev. Billy Sunday came to Columbus yesterday with a triumph that indicated he was returning to his own. He held twenty-five thousand persons in the hollow of his hand while he defied precedent and the physician's orders, and broke records for himself and for Columbus, addressing the largest single audience that ever sat under the spell of his voice.

" Olentangy Park was gay in its holiday dress. Merry-go-rounds and brass bands in the distance vied unsuccessfully for attention while the evangelist told the people assembled what he thought of ' Butterfly Chasers.'

" With his characteristic vigor he crowded the day full to overflowing. He had not taken a seat in the waiting auto, while the reception committee crowded around, before he announced that he wanted to speak at the penitentiary at nine-thirty. No one in Columbus had the slightest intimation of that intention, but there was nothing to do but to fall in with his plans. The address at the prison over, Mr. Sunday and his party were taken to the Railway Y. M. C. A., where a suite of rooms had been reserved for him, and where he made a pretext of resting in the intervals of receiving a stream of callers prior to the luncheon, at which a hundred men from the city and various parts of the state sat down.

" In conclusion Mr. Sunday was called upon for a few words, and in one of those rapid-fire addresses which consume exactly two minutes, by a stop watch, and are the despair of all stenographers, he told for himself and his party how Columbus had held a dear and tender spot in their hearts; how he was breaking a rule of seventeen years to come here, and how his heart had gone out to the city when he heard of the damage done by the flood.

" A few minutes later he was being whirled away to

Olentangy Park, while people along the way stood and waved at him, shouting welcomes and bidding him God-speed. Everywhere he went the experience was the same.

"While Mr. Sunday was being entertained by the men, Mrs. Sunday was the guest of the wives of the officers of the Northside Chamber of Commerce, at a luncheon in the Chittenden Hotel.

"The program of speeches at the park was turned topsy-turvy at the last minute. Governor Cox and Attorney-General Hogan were called out of the city, and Senator W. A. Greenlund, one of the speakers, had to leave the ground before Mr. Sunday concluded his address.

"About sixty thousand people crowded into the park. It was the largest gathering of this kind ever held in Columbus. Mr. Sunday's address was peculiarly replete with incident, epigram and anecdote, held together by a serious thread of thought, which first pointed and then shot home the truth that life is worth living if it is worthily lived, and that what people get and see depends largely upon their viewpoint and their contribution to life. During all of his campaign here the evangelist never appeared to better advantage than yesterday. As far as the uttermost vibration of his voice would reach people stood and listened, frequently laughing and applauding.

"It was Billy Sunday day. Try as they would to keep the May day outing to the fore, it was Billy Sunday that made the outing, and not the outing that got a hearing for Billy Sunday.

"The great meeting was brought to a close by a characteristic prayer on the part of the evangelist, who prayed for blessing on all present. On the city, state and county officials, and referring to the local campaign as probably the greatest awakening since the days of Pentecost.

" Mrs. Sunday also was lifted to the table, and said that she realized that her great mission in life was to take care of her husband, and that she was trying to do that to the best of her ability. She said she never would be able to express the sense of appreciation she had of the reception tendered her and her husband in Columbus.

" The extreme democracy of Sunday was shown upon his arrival, when he shook hands with all the men about the station and the Railway Y. M. C. A., where he went back into the kitchen and greeted the cook and all the waiters. Many sought to save the evangelist an imagined embarrassment by introducing people who had met him during the campaign, but in almost every instance this was a wasted effort, as he recalled practically every man and face without seeming effort."

It will also be quite proper to refer in this chapter to a notable demonstration that resulted from the great meeting held at Wilkes-Barre. As a result of awakened conscience following the campaign in that city, a public demonstration in the form of a law-and-order parade was held in Wilkes-Barre on Monday night, June 2, 1913, in which more than ten thousand people marched. Practically all these were men, with a small percentage of boys. There could be no doubt that this body of men was strictly in favor of enforcement of the Sunday closing law, etc.

The demonstration was out of the ordinary in many ways. There have seldom been as many men gathered in any city for such a purpose. Again, these were all men from the one county. The parade was also held at the close of a very busy day, when many men who would have taken part if possible were unable to get around from their evening meal.

There were thousands upon thousands of sympathetic people lining the streets for two miles of the line of march. The banners and songs prepared for the occasion left not the least doubt as to the sentiment of every one who participated in this great parade for decency and the honesty of public officials.

XXI

SOME PERSONAL MATTERS

IT may surprise many to learn that in private life Sunday is a very quiet man. He is so intensely active in his preaching, and so full of fire when holding a meeting, that many think he must be noisy at all times, but nothing could be more wide of the mark. With his great store of general information, his matured opinions upon nearly all subjects, and his ability to give clear expression to what he thinks, he could easily become a brilliant conversationalist, if he cared to, but he seems to prefer hearing others talk.

Those who have known him long say he has always been of a sensitive nature, and of quiet and retiring disposition. When with others he has little to say, but is one of the best of listeners. He never misses a word that is addressed to him, and shows his keen interest by his expression and attitude.

He also has a remarkable memory, and seems not to forget anything he hears or reads, especially if it has anything in it that will make "good sermon stuff." Even when among his most intimate friends, he lets them do most of the talking. He tells many stories in illustrating his sermons, and good ones, too, and he tells them with master strokes, but seldom or never does he tell a story in private conversation.

Sunday has a keen sense of humor, and enjoys hearing a good story as well as any one, but it must be clean in thought and language. He will not listen to anything that is at all questionable.

Billy is quite fastidious about his clothes. They must fit him " like the paper on the wall." He is never seen on the platform wearing anything that has the remotest suspicion of a wrinkle in it. He believes that some men are as divinely called to be tailors as he has been to preach, and so he allows the tape measure to be passed over his person only by the knight of the goose he is sure fills the bill on that line. It is because his tailor is an artist that everywhere, except at Winona Lake, Sunday always looks as though he had just stepped out of a fashion plate. How he looks at Winona is shown in one of the illustrations.

He generally carries a half-dozen suits with him, in a wardrobe trunk, that takes them through without a crease, and he sees to it that they are all kept pressed and ready to put on. He never wears a Prince Albert, or anything that gives him a preacher look. To have the preacher marks about him, he fears, might make some men take the other side of the street, and as a servant of God he wants to get as close to men as he can.

A few years ago he always wore a white vest, but now he is usually seen clad in a two-piece suit, with a belt. His linen is always immaculate, and his ties very neat and tasty, and harmonizing with his suit. He sweats so profusely when speaking that he has to buy expensive ties to prevent their being faded. His overcoat is about the only article of dress he ever puts on that has much weight, for he seems to abhor heavy clothing as he does a hypocrite, and sticks to light summer underwear all the year round, and yet he seems never to take cold.

One of Billy's strongest peculiarities is that he will not often use adhesive postage stamps in his correspondence.

To receive a letter with a stamp stuck to it, and purporting to come from him, would be certain to awaken distrust from any of his intimate friends. No psychologist has ever undertaken to give a scientific explanation of just why Sunday will not have anything to do with the gummed postage stamp, but the milk in the cocoanut is probably this:

In the days when a letter from the girl who is now Mrs. Sunday was due to reach him every day, and two on Monday, there were times, no doubt, when in spite of the best intention on the part of the sender, the stamp would come off, and if the creamy missive reached William at all, its beauty was marred by having "TWO CENTS DUE" smeared upon it with a rubber stamp, by a postal clerk who had no poetry in his soul, and which, considering the way Billy was "gone on Nell," must have greatly marred his enjoyment of the closely written eighteen scented pages, and postscript on a piece of curl paper he found inside.

But whether this is the correct surmise or not, the fact remains that Billy always keeps well stocked up with government envelopes, which have the stamp both embossed and printed in the grain, so that if the letter ever reaches its destination the stamp cannot be somewhere else.

Sunday shaves himself, and does it good and proper, too, with the same kind of a razor Noah had in the ark. He abominates a safety as a Turk does soap, and will have nothing to do with it. Those who live in the same house with him sometimes hear wails in the morning hour, that in their drowsy state make them dream that one of the domestics is doing penance for mortal sin, but they are soon sufficiently aroused to know that "it is only the boss in the bathroom shaving."

Sunday is good at drawing the blade, but he is not an artist at sharpening a razor, and as he will not wait a minute for anybody else to help him there, he makes up by main strength for what the razor lacks in edge, and so both he and those who want to sleep have to suffer the consequences. A more deliberate man than Billy would have a smoother time, in some ways, and so would his friends.

Sunday has had many experiences that do not come to all of us. When a little fellow out in Iowa, he was one day having a small boy's time in "the old swimmin' hole," when he got beyond his depth, and was so nearly drowned that it took all the neighbors and the hardest kind of work to bring him to. He still remembers the experience with a shudder, and says the common impression that drowning is a most delightful death to die is all bunk. He wouldn't go through it again, he says, for anything you could name. He would rather shave.

In the summer of 1909 he made a trip with Glenn Curtiss, in an aeroplane, and that he remembers as beating drowning forty laps for delight. "That was something worth while! Interesting? You're talking. Something doing every minute; and as for thrills—a half-dozen at once sometimes—and then some. The ascension was made at Winona Lake, and the sail around over the lake, high enough to get a magnificent view reaching a long distance, and not too high up to see things below distinctly—it was great! It was a wonderful—wonderful experience; to climb up into the air, and see the beautiful world God has given to us, as the birds see it! Think of it!"

He says the sentence, "They shall mount up with wings as eagles," was always a favorite promise of his, but he never expected to see it so literally fulfilled as it was in his case.

One of Sunday's experiences that proved to be a most unpleasant one, occurred at Springfield, Ill. One evening, soon after the beginning of the meeting, a man who was afterward found to be insane, made a vicious attack upon him with a wagon whip, just after he had announced his text and begun to preach. With the subtle cunning which is so characteristic of the insane, the man had managed to elude the ushers, and smuggle himself and his great whip into a seat well to the front. Watching his chance, he sprang forward, almost with the speed of light, and gave Sunday one most vicious cut over the legs below the knees. But before he could raise his arm to strike another blow, Sunday jumped from his high platform upon the man, and knocked him down as he descended. Sunday was not much hurt by the whip, but in the jump his ankle was sprained so badly that he had to go on crutches for several weeks, but he never missed a night service.

Billy has all sorts of experiences with people who are off in their minds, and gets anonymous letters almost by the hatful, from some of the crankiest cranks anybody ever had to deal with. All such letters go into the waste basket without a second glance.

Sunday is a man of many moods, and those who would get on well with him need to learn to read them as a sailor does the weather signs. He is as finely organized as a thoroughbred racer, and is of such a strongly nervous temperament that he is as sensitive to surrounding conditions as a thermometer. He has fine health, and is always ready for every duty that presents itself. If he ever had a regular spell of sickness, or missed a speaking date through illness, the knowledge of it has never reached this writer. He seems not to require much sleep, and yet there are times in certain stages of a meeting when he does not sleep as well as he should. There are times in every campaign when the burden upon him from the meeting is terrific. There is so much at stake, and so multitudinous are the cares and details, and so disastrous would be the result should essential things not be properly looked after, that sleep is sometimes hardest to obtain when needed the most.

It is doubtful if any other evangelist was ever so good a sleeper as Moody. He made it a lifelong habit never to sap his energy by the slightest friction of worry. He believed that if he did the best he knew, and did his work the best he was able, the Lord could be trusted to carry all the burden, and that is why he could go on his way in light marching order. But we must remember that, in their mental and physical makeup, Moody and Sunday were the opposite of each other.

Moody did his work at a deliberate walk, while Sunday does his on the run, for the spirit of the age has taken hold of him. Moody never ran a footrace, even to make a train, while Sunday was a sprinter from his babyhood. Both were ever intensely in earnest, and each with a consuming passion for souls, but being so opposite in character their zeal found vent in quite different ways.

While in a meeting at Steubenville, Ohio, and several weeks before the beginning of the campaign at Pittsburg, Sunday and his party went over to Pittsburg, to have a meeting with the ministers who had given him a call. When Sunday was introduced he called up the different members of his party, one after another, and asked each one to tell the ministers all about his or her part of the work. The information thus given created much interest and surprise on the part of the preachers, not many of whom knew much about the magnitude and extent of the work. In this way every preacher present was quickly enabled to see what a tremendous sweep the movement is certain to have in a city. After all the others had spoken, and answered all the questions propounded to them, " Ma " Sunday was called to the platform, and also introduced by her husband. She brought down the house in the very first breath, by saying—

" And my work is to sit on the safety valve."

Then in a pertinent little speech that was full of good hits and plenty of information, the preachers of Pittsburg were speedily made to see that " Ma " Sunday's part in the great movement is far from being a sinecure.

No one could long be associated with Sunday without making the discovery that being famous has its drawbacks. Living in the limelight has its advantages, to be sure, and very great ones they are too, sometimes, but it also has its drawbacks, and nobody knows it better than Billy Sunday. It is not always the flower-strewn path, arched with rainbows and carpeted with velvet, that those of us who dwell in the valley of humility may suppose it to be. One of the trying things about it is, that if you do anything that lifts you above the common level, you can't turn around without having people everywhere put on their nose glasses to stare at you. Lion hunters everywhere will get after you, and chase you up hill and down without mercy.

The famous man is regarded as public property everywhere. On the street, in the store, on the train, in the hotel or private home, people will hold their breath and stand still to look at him. If he smiles they will look tickled, and if he frowns they will look serious and shake their heads in great solemnity.

It is said that in Japan whenever an American goes to his room all the neighbors will surround the house and punch holes through the paper walls with their fingers, through which to stare at him. A fate something like that follows the famous man in this country wherever he goes. People with eyes like X-rays are always springing out upon him. There is no retirement, no seclusion for him. Wherever he goes somebody is sure to recognize him and let the cat out of the bag, and then there is no rest for the weary.

If Sunday were to meet all the people who press upon him for interviews when he is in the midst of a campaign, he would have no time or opportunity for anything else. And most of those who thus want to see him have no business with him whatever. They may have heard him preach somewhere, years ago, perhaps, and believe it will make him shouting happy for them to call and tell him so.

Sunday shrinks from being lionized, and never feels so ill at ease as when people gushingly praise him to his face, and yet he would not under any consideration say or do anything that would in the slightest way lessen his influence for good with any one. It is because of this that he often gives up the opportunity for much needed rest to meet urgent calls for interviews.

Tens of thousands of people have been converted through Sunday's instrumentality, and hosts of these feel that they have a strong personal interest in him, and in whatever belongs to him. That is why great throngs go to see his home at Winona Lake, and it is also the reason that none who call are ever turned away without being courteously shown over the house, even in the absence of the family.

SERMONS

By William A. Sunday

THE THREE GROUPS

Lord, is it I?—Matt. 26:22.

GOD created man and placed him in the Garden of Eden, and gave him an explicit command, and man disobeyed, with the full knowledge of the penalty ringing in his ears, for God said: "In the day thou eatest of the fruit thou shalt surely die."

The Lord did not mean a period of twenty-four hours, but did mean that man would pass a crisis in his career. Adam ate of the forbidden fruit, and this world became a graveyard. If man had not sinned we never would have died. All the misery, all the disease, all the heartaches have come through sin. The hearse backs up in front of our homes and drives away with our loved ones because of sin.

But when man sinned God gave the promise, "The seed of the woman shall bruise the serpent's head." In the fullness of time Jesus came into the world in fulfillment of that promise. He opened the eyes of the blind, stilled the tempest, fed the multitude with five loaves and two fishes, cast out devils and raised the dead. He demonstrated by word and deed that He was the Son of God. The Jews spurned and repudiated His claim. and their enmity finally culminated in His crucifixion. But before that heartrending tragedy was enacted several incidents occurred, from one of which I take my text.

Jesus said to His disciples, "Go your way into the

village over against you, and you will find a colt tied, whereon never man sat; loose him and bring him to Me. And if any man ask you, Why do ye this? say, The Lord hath need of him; and straightway he will send him hither." And the disciples went their way and found the colt tied in front of a house where two ways met, and there was a crowd of men loafing about the place; and if they were in any way like the bunch in our day, they were whittling, cursing, chewing tobacco, discussing financial, political and all other public questions.

The disciples began untying the colt, when one fellow, who spits tobacco juice enough to drown a rabbit, calls out, " Hey there! What are you doing? What are you going to do with that colt?" The disciples call back: " The Lord hath need of him." So away they go with the colt to where Jesus was and He on its back enters the city of Jerusalem on His famous triumphal entry.

A great multitude followed, shouting, " Hosanna to the son of David! Blessed is He that cometh in the name of the Lord!" They spread their garments on the ground in front of Jesus. They cut down branches from the trees; they paved His way with flowers. You would have thought by their acclaim that then and there they would crown Him, but let us wait and see.

Jesus said to Peter and John, " You go on, and you will meet a man bearing a pitcher of water. You follow him into the house he enters, and say to the goodman of the house, ' Where is the guest chamber?' He will show you an upper room furnished; there make ready."

Jesus desired to eat the Passover feast with His disciples, commemorating the passing over of the destroying angel, who went throughout the land of Egypt and slew the first-born in every home where the blood was not on the doorposts. That night at the table Peter noticed that Jesus looked sad and troubled. Turning to John, who was one of the favored disciples, he said, "Ask Him what's the matter?" John said, "Master, you look worried. Why is it?" Jesus replied: "One of you shall betray me." Peter asked, in the words of my text: "Lord, is it I?" John also asked: "Lord, is it I?" And Judas, the arch traitor, had the cheek and the audacity to look Jesus in the face and ask: "Lord, is it I?" When for days he had been bartering and bickering to betray Jesus to the Pharisees for thirty pieces of silver; or about fifteen dollars and ninety-five cents in our money.

Jesus replied: "It is he to whom I give the sop." So saying, He dipped it in the dish and handed the sop to Judas, saying: "That thou doest, do quickly." Pricked to the heart by the words of Jesus, Judas leaped to his feet, and because he was treasurer of the little apostolic band, seizing the money bag, he left the room.

And when they had sung an hymn Jesus, with the remaining eleven disciples, went out and crossed the brook Kedron and entered into the Garden of Gethsemane. This brings me to the subject of my sermon: The Three Groups in the Garden.

I. DIFFERENCE IN POSITION:

They were not grouped by their rating in Bradstreet or Dun. Every man classified himself; and you do the same. You are where you are because Jesus knows He cannot trust you in a more responsible place. Judas classified himself with the enemies of God.

The first group was near the edge of the garden; the second group farther in the garden, while Jesus, we are told, was a stone's throw farther on. The first group

of disciples was so near the edge of the garden that they
would have had only a short distance to go to have
been outside where Judas was, with the scribes,
Pharisees and the mob.

I am sorry to say it, but it's the truth. The truth is
not always pleasant to hear, but it's profitable for all
who will profit by the truth. The first group is analogous
to the position of a large percentage of members in the
average church to-day. They live such a selfish, indifferent, apathetic, "good Lord, good devil," milk and
chalk, cider and vinegar sort of a life that it's hard to
tell whether they are in the church or in the world. I
detest any man who will trim his sails to catch a passing
breeze of popularity, and fight under a doubtful flag.
I love to see a person come clear out for God without
compromise.

The nearer the relationship the stronger are the ties
of obligation. I owe to Mrs. Sunday and our children
that which I do not owe to any other woman or children
in the world, because of my relationship. You owe to
your wife and children that which you do not owe to
any other beings. I owe to Jesus that which I do not
owe to the world. I testify of the world that its deeds
are evil. I do not care whether they hiss me or applaud
me; whether they dine me or damn me. Jesus said:
"The world will hate you as it hateth Me." "Woe unto
thee when all men speak well of thee." One of the
most uncomplimentary things that can be said at your
funeral, is that you had no enemies. If you live an
uncompromising life for Christ you will have enemies.

The nearer the relationship the greater the provoca-
tion. I could in one act break my wife's heart, and
bring disgrace upon my children, but that act would not
put a tear in your eye. Why? Because all the interest

Churches want MORE GOD

LESS DRESS = STRIFE = MONEY = SOCIAL LIFE

ILLUS. WOMAN LINCOLN

II. DIFFERENCE SIZE

Most glorious exploits not always furnish
clearest index vice--virtue--etc/

Sometimes look--word--presence - WEBSTER

Talk with Jesus How many disciples? HAD 12--ONE GONE ASTRAY JUDAS BOUGHT TICKET HELL 30 pieces silver NOT ROUND-TRIP EITHER	Talk with the LIGHT WHERE JESUS? DON'T KNOW " P. J. JNo. " " " JUDAS? " " WENT PAST SANHEDRIN

JESUS GONE MT. TRANS. P. J. JOHN

DEVIL CAUSE SALooN-SHAME
DRUNK - THIEF-
PANDERER Etc

FATHER BOY POSSESSED WITH DEVIL CAME TO 8
Is father here never had trouble boy?
This father weighted trouble--child--devil

YET SOME PEOPLE THINK THROWING STONES THEM to SPEAK
AGAINST THE DEVIL.

SAY "OLD DEVIL PAYS WAY LET STAY"   NEED SALooNS

LICENSE GET SALOON--PAVES STREET, etc. KEEP PEN. JAIL

EVERY SALOON GIVES DEVIL CHANCE GET BOY PooR H. INSANE

IF WANT WORLD BETTER AFTER WHILE KEEP THE DEVIL OUT BOY
DRIVE DEVIL OUT - HIT HIM CRADLE = NoT CRUTcH
Brought to disciples Could cast out
CARD-PLAYING--DANCING CROWD CAST NO DEVIL

A SINGLE SHEET FROM MR. SUNDAY'S SERMON NOTES.

you have toward me is that I may entertain or instruct you, and perhaps your concern ends there.

I have imagined that the conduct of multitudes who are in the church must almost break the heart of Christ. God has the right to say, " I did not send My Son into the world to bathe it in blood and tears, and open His veins with the cruel instrument of the cross, to redeem you to serve the flesh and the devil, but to serve Me. I want your influence, your time, your money, your prayers, your tears."

Alexander the Great was once asked to engage in the Olympic games. He replied: " I will, if kings are to be mine antagonists on the race track." If we were found doing nothing in this world that is not in harmony with our birth from above we would move this old sin-soaked world Godward. You cannot do as you please. The higher you climb the plainer you are seen. When you are away from home, don't forget that God is everywhere.

When the son of Fulvius was discovered with the conspirators of Catiline, his old father rebuked him by saying: " I did not beget thee to serve Catiline, but to serve your country—Rome! " You are redeemed by the precious blood of Christ, not to serve the world, but to serve God.

I love to see people as loyal to Jesus as was Speaker Lenthall to the Constitution in the days of King Charles I. When commanded to dissolve Parliament, he said: " I have neither eyes to see, ears to hear, nor tongue to speak, but as the Constitution, whose servant I am, is pleased to direct me." Or as Prince William of Orange was to the Netherlands in the thirty-seven years of war. King Philip of Spain offered him fabulous sums to surrender. Prince William sent back that message which has become mosaiced in the hearts of the Dutch people: "Not for life nor wife, nor children, nor lands would I mix in my cup one drop of the poison of treason!" No wonder, that when he was slain by the hand of an assassin, little children stopped playing and cried.

Many of our churches are not much more than mere social organizations. They spend more time in developing along social lines than along spiritual lines. Business men and influential church members do not do their duty; they are completely wrapped up in their own affairs. They are busy with the pursuits and frivolities of the world, and they lose the track. The old-time fire and the old-time spirit are lacking. What can we expect from a social club other than a leading away from God? Our churches need more of God; less of dress, strife after wealth, and social life.

A woman in a western city went to her pastor and asked: "What can I do to win my husband to Christ?" He answered: "You cannot win anyone to Christ the way you live." She hung her head in shame and went home.

When her husband and her son, a young man of eighteen, came home, she said to them: "I wish you would remain a little while after dinner. I want to speak with you." They stepped into the parlor, and she put an arm about each and said: "I have not been a consistent Christian, therefore I feel I have not been as good a wife to you, husband, or as good a mother to you, son, as I should have been. Will you join me in prayer that God will forgive me?" They all three kneeled, and she tried to pray, but all she could say was, "O God! O God!" But the Spirit broke up the fountains of the deep, and all three wept. A few days later her husband publicly accepted Christ and joined the church.

"Husband, tell me why I couldn't win you to Christ before?" she asked, and he said: "I would ask you to go with me to the theater, and you would go; to the dance, and you would go; to play cards, and you would. You drank wine with me. Then you would ask me to go to church with you, and to prayer meeting, and I would go. You went where I went, and I went where you went. You did what I did, and I did what you did. Wherein was your life any better than mine?"

To be able to convict others of sin, we must ourselves first get right with God.

II. DIFFERENCE IN SIZE:

Eight in the first group. Three in the second group. Jesus alone forms the third. The largest number in the first group. Farthest from Jesus. Nearest to the world. That has always been true of every church that I knew anything about. Ask the minister for a list of his members; then sit down and check off the prayer meeting members. You will find the largest number nearer the card party and wine supper; closer to the world than to the cross of Christ. Somebody said to Daniel Webster when he was a boy: "What are you going to be when you are a man?" "A lawyer," he replied. "But the profession is overrun." Webster answered: "There is plenty of room at the top." The nearer you get to Jesus the more elbow room you will have and the less the crowd. The most glorious exploits do not always furnish us with the clearest index of the vices or virtues of men and women. Sometimes a word, an act, a gesture; your absence or your presence will give a clearer insight into your manhood or womanhood, or lack of both, than some deed of bravery or act of prowess.

Let us talk with Jesus a minute. "Jesus, how many disciples have you?" "I had twelve. I have but eleven now." "Where is the missing one?" "He has gone to betray Me." "And yet with eleven left you are praying all alone?" Just like many a minister with hundreds of members, and bearing the burden all alone.

Judas bought a ticket for hell for thirty pieces of silver, and it wasn't a round-trip ticket either. Let us go talk with the eight:

"Where is Jesus?" "We don't know." "Where are Peter, James and John?" "Don't know; haven't seen them." "Where is Judas?" "Why, he just went past not long ago, with the scribes and Pharisees and a great company." "Where was he going?" "Why, he was looking for Jesus, to betray Him." "Why do you think that?" "Because to-night at the feast Jesus said, 'One of you shall betray Me, and it is he to whom I give the sop,' and after dipping it in the dish He handed it to Judas." "Didn't you try to stop him in his dastardly work of betrayal?" "No." "Well, don't you suppose Judas thought he would find Jesus here with you men?"

No, he never suspected that Jesus was near that bunch. Judas knew that crowd. He knew that first group out near the edge of the garden through and through. Why do I think so? I will tell you. Jesus had gone up on the mount of transfiguration, taking with him Peter, James and John, members of the second group, and while He was away a father whose boy was possessed with a devil came to the disciples who composed the first group, out near the edge of the garden, and besought them to cast the devil out of his boy.

Jesus had given His disciples power against unclean spirits, to drive them out, but instead of doing the work

He gave them to do, they spent the time chewing the rag about who would be greatest in the kingdom.

I wonder if there is a father in this world who never had trouble with his boy. This father was weighted down with trouble all caused by the devil. The devil is the cause of every saloon, every drunkard, every murder, every theft, every lie, every heartache, every house of shame. All of the deception, envy, malice, filthy communications that come out of your mouth are prompted by the devil, and yet some people think I am throwing stones at them when I preach against the devil.

Some say, " Well, the devil pays, so let him stay. We need the license from the saloons to pave our streets and light our city." Yes, and you need your saloons in order to keep your jails, penitentiaries, poorhouses and insane asylums filled. Every saloon gives the devil that much better chance to get your boy.

If you want the world to be better after a while, keep the devil out of the boys and girls. If you want to drive the devil out of the world, hit him with a cradle, not a crutch.

When Jesus returned from the mount the sorrowing father ran to Him with his boy, crying, " If Thou canst do anything, have compassion on us, and help us. I brought my son to Thy disciples, and they could not cast the devil out! "

That " if " implies a doubt. Failure on the part of those disciples to keep in touch with Jesus, so they could have power to cast out devils, led the poor old father to doubt the power of Jesus. The divine philosophy, as demonstrated by thousands of church members, breeds more infidels than all the Paines, Parkers and Ingersolls combined.

As a principle increases in its meaning, it decreases in

the number that should adhere to that principle. Suppose by education I mean every one who can read and write; then there are about eighty-five millions of educated people in the United States. But, suppose that by education I mean every one who has graduated from high school; about one-fifth of the population would be classified as educated. On the other hand, if by education I mean every one who has graduated from a university or a college; one-half of one per cent. would come under that heading.

Suppose by your friends you mean all who shake your hand, smile and say, "How are you? I am glad to see you." You have scores of friends of that sort; but suppose by friends you mean all who will stand by you through thick and thin, and defend you when they hear your name defamed, I fear they are lamentably few. Suppose by a Christian I mean every one who has his name on a church record; there are about twenty-six millions in the United States, about equally divided between the Catholics and Protestants. On the other hand, suppose I mean every man and woman who is willing to do God's will; I question whether there are ten millions that would die for Jesus.

I said to a minister one time, "How many members have you?" He said, "Eight hundred and seventy-two; but there are two hundred and seventy-eight I do not count." I asked: "Out of the number you do count, how many are helping in the meetings: singing in the choir, ushering or doing personal work?" Tears flowed down his cheeks as he said, the largest number I have been able to muster any one night was twenty-eight, and if my life depended on my making the number fifty, I would die!"

There we were wearing out our lives, trying to bring

that God-forsaken, whisky-soaked, gambling-cursed, har-
lot-blighted town to her knees, and the church calmly
looking on. I sometimes doubt whether the church needs
new members one-half as much as she needs the old
bunch made over. Judging by the way multitudes in
the church live, you would think they imagined they
had a through ticket to heaven in a Pullman palace car,
and had left orders for the porter to wake them up when
they head into the yards of the New Jerusalem. If
that's the case you will be doomed to disappointment,
for you will be side-tracked with a hot box.

If I had a hundred tongues, and every tongue speaking a different language, in a different key at the same
time, I could not do justice to the splendid chaos that
the world-loving, dancing, card-playing, whisky-guzzling,
gin-fizzling, wine-sizzling, novel-reading crowd in the
church brings to the cause of Christ. There is but one
voice from faithful preacher and worker about the
church, and that is, " She is sick," but we say it in such
painless, delicate terms that she seems to enjoy her in-
validity. About four out of five who have their names
on our church records are doing nothing to bring the
world to Christ, and the church is not one whit better
for their presence. As a satisfaction for all this, Christians are making a great deal out of Lent. I believe in
a Lent that is kept three hundred and sixty-five days
in the year. I think it a travesty on the teachings of
Christ that any one can get such an overstock of piety
on hands in forty days they can live like the devil the
rest of the year. That's an old trick of the devil.

The Jewish church struck that rock and was wrecked.
The Roman Catholic church struck and was split. The
Protestant church is fast approaching the same doom.
One of the great dangers, as I see it, is assimilation to

the world; the neglect of the poor; substitution of forms
for the facts of godliness; a hireling ministry, all summed
up, means a fashionable church, with religion left out.

Formerly Methodists attended class meeting and gave
testimony; now the class meeting has become a thing of
the past. Shouts of praise used to be heard. Now such
holy demonstrations are considered undignified. Occasionally some godly old sister, who is a sort of a con-
necting link between the old and the new, pipes up in
a weak, negative falsetto, apologetic kind of a voice,
and says:

" Amen, Brother Sunday! "

I don't expect one of these ossified, petrified, mil-
dewed, dyed-in-the-wool, stamped-on-the-cork, blown-in-
the-bottle, horizontal, perpendicular Presbyterians or
Episcopalians to shout " Amen! " but it would do you
good to loosen up. Many of you are hide-bound.

I believe half of the professing Christians amount to
nothing as a spiritual force. They go to church, have
a kindly regard for religion, but as for having a firm
grip on God, a cheerful spirit of self-denial, enthusiastic
service and prevailing prayer, and willingness to strike
hard, staggering blows against the devil, they are almost
failures. A shell has been invented which, when it
strikes a ship, puts everybody on board to sleep. Some
such thing seems to have hit our churches.

III. DIFFERENCE IN REVELATION:

Jesus said to the members of the first group, near the
edge of the garden, largest in numbers, " Sit ye here."
To those composing the second, He said, " My soul is
exceeding sorrowful, even unto death. Tarry ye here,
and watch with Me. Watch and pray, lest ye enter into
temptation. The spirit truly is willing, but the flesh is

weak." But when He was alone He cried, "Father, if it be possible, let this cup pass from Me: nevertheless, not My will, but Thine, be done."

Notice the progressive stages of revelation. Not a word to Judas. To the eight nearest the world, He said, "Sit ye here." To Peter, James and John, He said, "Watch and pray." When alone with the Father, "Thy will be done." He told the Father what He did not tell Peter, James and John. He told them what He did not tell the group of eight; what He did not tell Judas. Do you wish God to reveal the deep things of the Spirit to you? Then turn your back on the sinful things and creep close to His side.

Jesus will never unfold His revelations to you when you are lined up in front of a bar drinking, or when you are at a baseball game on the Sabbath, or living in sin. Jesus did not ask the members of the first group, near the edge of the garden, to pray. Perhaps they would have refused. Every minister knows there are certain members of his church that he never thinks of asking to lead in prayer. In fact they never darken a prayer meeting door; if a card party takes place on prayer meeting night they are at the party. Yet we wonder why this old sin-blighted world is not on her knees. I am amazed that God is doing as well as He is, with the crowd He has to work with.

Please pardon a personal reference: I was born and bred, not in Old Kentucky, although my grandfather was born in Lexington, but in Old Iowa. I was a rube of the rubes, a hayseed of the hayseeds. I have greased my hair with goose grease. I have blacked my boots with stove blacking. I have wiped my face on a gunny-sack towel. I have eaten with my knife. I have drank coffee out of my saucer. I have said "done it," when

I should have said, "did it;" "came," when I should
have said, "come"; "seen," when I should have said,
"saw." I am a graduate from the university of poverty
and hard knocks, and I have taken post-graduate courses.
My autobiography could be summed up in one line from
Gray's "Elegy": "The short and simple annals of the
poor."

My father enlisted four months before I was born.
He went to the front with Company E, Twenty-third Iowa
Infantry, but he never came back. He died and was
buried at Camp Patterson, Mo. I have battled my way
since I was six years old. I know all about the dark
and seamy side of life. If ever a man fought hard every
inch of his way, I have.

One day mother said, "Boys, I am going to send you
to the Soldiers' Orphans' Home at Glenwood, Iowa."
We had to go to Ames to take the train. We went to
a little hotel to wait, and about one o'clock some one
came and said, "Get ready for the train; it's coming."

I looked into mother's face. Her eyes were red;
her hair was disheveled. I said, "What's the matter,
mother?" All the time Ed and I slept mother had been
praying. We went to the train. Mother put one arm
about me and the other about Ed, and sobbed as if her
heart would break. People walked by and looked at us,
but they didn't say a word. Why? They didn't know,
and if they had they wouldn't have cared. Mother knew;
she knew that for years she wouldn't see her boys.

We got into the train and cried, "Good-by, mother!"
as the train pulled out. We reached Council Bluffs. It
was cold, and we turned up our little thin coat collars
over our necks and shivered. We saw a hotel, and
went up and asked a woman for something to eat. She
said, "What's your name?" "My name is Willie Sun-

day, and this is my brother Ed," I said. "Where are you going?" "Going to the Soldiers' Orphans' Home at Glenwood." She wiped her tears and said, "My husband was a soldier, and he never came back. He wouldn't turn any one away, and I certainly won't turn you boys away." She threw her arms about us and said, "Come on in." She gave us our breakfast, and our dinner too.

There wasn't any train going out on the Burlington until afternoon. We played around the yards. We saw a freight train standing there, so we climbed into the caboose. The conductor came along and said, "Where is your money?" "Ain't got any." "Where's your tickets?" "Ain't got any." "You can't ride without money or tickets. I'll have to put you off."

We commenced to cry. My brother handed him a letter of introduction to the superintendent of the Orphans' Home. The conductor read it, handed it back as the tears rolled down his cheeks; then said: "Just sit still, boys. It won't cost you a cent to ride on my train."

It's only twenty miles from Council Bluffs to Glenwood, and as we rounded the curve the conductor said, "There is the Home on the hill."

Mother knew. Ed didn't know. I didn't know. I went to sleep. So did Ed; but mother knew. She prayed.

Jesus knew. He prayed. Peter, James and John went to sleep. You can't make me believe that if you knew you would act as you do. If you will tell me how much you read the Bible, how much you pray, how much you do to help people to Jesus Christ, I will tell you to what figures you point on the spiritual thermometer. The trouble is, you will be in the church on Sunday morning, and will keep a little spot about eighteen inches square warm for half an hour; listen to the sermon; pick up a book and sing, "Jesus paid it all," when you have debts that are outlawed. He doesn't pay them. He doesn't pay for that hat, or that set of false teeth you are wearing. You get up and say, "I am standing on the solid rock." You are probably standing in a pair of shoes you haven't paid for yet. Let's get cleaned up for God, and see if the Lord won't do great things. He will not send the wind to drive our ships unless we have faith to lift our sails.

IV. DIFFERENCE IN DUTY:

To the members of the first group Jesus said, "Sit ye here." To those of the second group He said, "Watch and pray." While His duty was to bear the sins of the world, there are multitudes in the church that do nothing. They are mere ciphers. At a funeral the preacher failed to appear. The undertaker thought it would be a downright shame to put the man away without something being said, and so concluded to make a few remarks himself. So when the time came he cleared his throat, and in a pious whine said: "Dear friends, this corpse has been a member of this church for forty years!"

"Crucify Him!" cried the relentless rabble. The vociferations of that infuriated mob shook the temple from foundation to turret top. Often in civil strife had been witnessed some such animosity and hatred of the multitudes. Truly all the phantoms of hell seem to have assembled in Jerusalem, and out through the funeral gate poured the mob.

Here comes Judas, leading the devil's crowd. Turning to the Pharisees, he said, "Whomsoever I shall kiss, that same is He; hold Him fast." See the smile on his hypocritical, sanctimonious countenance, as he rushes forward shouting, "Hail, Master!" and kisses Him.

Jesus answers, " Judas, betrayest thou the Son of man with a kiss?"

They seize Him. and take Him to the High Priest's house, where He is condemned on false testimony to a felon's death on the cross.

> "Must Jesus bear the cross alone,
>   And all the world go free?
> No! There's a cross for every one,
>   And there's a cross for me."

As one has beautifully pictured the scene, by saying he imagined that had we been there, and God had given us power of vision, we might have seen the hilltops covered with angels, and the air filled with the heavenly hosts, all gazing breathless upon that scene. The archangel opened the door of heaven, and cried:

"O Jesus! if you want me to come to your help, raise your head and look this way; and I will come with a legion of angels to your help!" But Jesus suffered on. He imagined the archangel once more leaning over the battlements of heaven, and crying again, with a voice that shook the earth:

"O Jesus! thou Son of God! If you want me to come and hurl that howling, bloodthirsty mob into hell, tear your right hand loose from the cross and wave it!" But Jesus clenched His fingers over the nails in His hands and suffered on. Why? To open up a plan of salvation which, if we will accept, will keep us out of hell.

Suddenly He cried: "It is finished!" and the Holy Spirit plucked the olive branch of peace from the cross, and winging His flight back burst through the gates of glory, shouting: "Peace! Peace! Peace! has been made through His death on the cross."

How many will go with Jesus to the last ditch? Thousands will; but there are many who, like the disciples, follow Him to the Garden, but forsake Him at the Cross. How many will say with Jesus, " Not my will, but Thine be done." Say it with me: " Not my will, but——" finish the sentence. All the peace, all the power, all the blessing of a Christian life and eternal joy are found in the three words you have left out—" Thine be done." It costs some too much to say, " Thine be done." One says, " If I say that the saloon-keepers won't come to my store to trade. If I said that I would have to close my store on the Sabbath." " If I said that I could not accept Mrs. So-and-So's invitation to a card party." " If I said that I would have to pay my debts." " If I said that I would have to go home and burn up the prizes I have won at progressive euchre." " If I said that I could not go to the brothel any more and crawl into the arms of infamy." " If I should say, ' Thy will be done ' I should have to throw the wine out of my cellar and break up my beer bottles. I am going to have a few bottles for dinner to-night." " I could not go to the ball game on Sunday afternoon if I said that." " I would have to stop lying about my neighbors if I said that." Oh, yes, it costs too much to say " Thine be done." That is the reason you lose out. That's the reason you have moral curvature of the spine. That's the reason your spiritual batting average is not up to God's league standard.

" Not my will, but——" there's where you cash in. There's where you go into the ditch. There's where you turn off the light. There's where you hang up the receiver. There's where you ring off. There's where you puncture your tire. There's where you strike out. It costs too much to say, " Thine be done."

" Say, papa, may I go with you?" asked a little boy of his father.

" Yes, son, come on," said the father, as he threw the ax over his shoulder, and, accompanied by a friend, went to the woods and felled a tree. The little fellow said:

" Say, papa, can I go and play in the water in the lagoon?"

" Yes, but be careful, and don't get into the deep water; keep close to the bank."

The little fellow was playing, digging wells, picking up stones and shells, and talking to himself, when pretty soon the father heard him cry:

" Hurry, papa, hurry!"

The father leaped to his feet, grabbed the ax and ran to the lagoon and saw the boy floundering in deep water, with hands outstretched, a look of horror on his face, as he cried:

" Hurry, papa, hurry; the alligator has got me!"

The hideous, amphibious monster had been hibernating, and had come out, lean, lank, hungry, voracious, and seized the boy. The father leaped into the lagoon and was just about to sink the ax through the head of the monster, when he turned and swished the water with his huge tail like the screw of an ocean steamer, and the little fellow cried out:

" Hurry, papa, hurry!"

The blood-flecked foam told the story.

When I read that. for days I could not eat, for nights I could not sleep. I said:

" O God, what if that had been my boy!"

There are influences in this world worse than an alligator, and they are ripping and tearing to shreds our virtue, our morality. Young men are held by intemperance; others by vice. Drunkards are crying to 1 church, "Hurry faster!" and the church members on the bank playing cards, sit there drinking beer a reading novels.

"Hurry!"

They are splitting hairs over fool things, instead trying to keep sinners out of hell!

"Faster! Faster! Faster!"

"Lord, is it I?"

MEETING FOR " MEN ONLY "——COLUMBUS, O. THOUSANDS UNABLE TO GAIN ADMITTANCE.

UNDER THE SUN

What profit hath a man of all his labor which he taketh under the sun?—Eccl. 1:3.

THIS question is asked and answered by King Solomon, and in our language it means about this: "What good does a man get out of life if he lives only for what this world can give?"

If any man has ever been able to give the right answer to this great question, out of his own wisdom and experience, that man was Solomon. If any man ever came into this world with a gold spoon in his mouth, he certainly did. The devil has a mortgage on some people from the cradle, but Solomon had no such handicap, for he was well born. He was the favorite son of one of the greatest and best men who ever lived, for his father, King David, was a man after God's own heart—which means that he just suited the Lord.

Solomon was made king of a great kingdom in his early manhood, while his father was still alive to counsel and help him. From this we see that he had every advantage that high station and boundless wealth and opportunity could give him. He had wisdom, riches, wealth and honor such as no king ever had before him or since.

An invincible army stood ready to do his bidding, and all the power of a great nation that was under the especial protection and favor of God was behind him. He had only to command, and it was done; to express a wish, and it was gratified. He had received the best education it was possible to give him, and was called the wisest of men. The fame of his wisdom covered the earth, and caused the Queen of Sheba, with a great retinue, to make a long pilgrimage of weary weeks and months, to sit at his feet in wonder. She looked upon the beauty of his wonderful palace and the magnificent temple he had built. She reviewed his matchless army, considered the numbers of men who served him and the elegance of their livery; then she looked in amazement upon the wealth of gold and precious things that surrounded him, and took her departure, declaring that the half had not been told her.

This is the kind of ability Solomon had with which to answer his own question. He wrote three thousand proverbs and a thousand and five songs, all full of wisdom. If he wasn't qualified to speak as an expert, where can we find one?

Let us see how well qualified he was to know what he was talking about from his own actual experience. Every great pleasure was at his finger-tips. If he wanted anything he had only to reach out his soft, jeweled hand and take it. His kingdom had peace and rest from war during all of his reign, so that he had plenty of time to enjoy himself. And from what he says of himself he lost no time, for he took about all the degrees and invented a few of his own. He was a thirty-third degree sport.

He lived in a palace, surrounded by courtiers who were not spring chickens, and all highbrows themselves. He was honored, admired and flattered as few men have been. No greater honor than his could be known, no greater wisdom found in any books, and no higher station attained. He was so rich that his wealth could not be measured. He had forty thousand horses and twenty thousand horsemen. The high cost of living never troubled him, for his provisions for his household and attendants one day were: Two hundred and eighty-one bushels of fine flour; five hundred and sixty-six bushels of meal; ten fat oxen out of the stall; twenty oxen out of the pasture; one hundred sheep, besides harte, roebuck, fallow deer and fatted fowl.

Solomon had no ambition that had not been achieved; no curiosity that had not been satisfied. Like his princely father, he was a close observer, and nothing escaped him, so that he was able to say: " I have seen all the works that are done under the sun," meaning that the world had nothing more to show him or to give him—and that was certainly going some.

At some time in our lives we have all envied men of great scholarship and intellectual attainments, and have thought of what a foretaste of heaven it would be to have the time and opportunity to learn all the things we would like to know. We have believed that one of the greatest joys this life could give is the joy of knowing things. Well, Solomon not only drank that well dry, but he pulled out the pump, for he exhausted all the schools and colleges of his day, and gave all his teachers nervous prostration in their vain endeavor to teach him something more than he already knew. And then when he had pumped that fountain dry, he sighed and said: " Go to, now; I will see what I can get out of mirth and pleasure," and then he cut loose on that line, and began to carry on in a way to make a baseball fan at the world's series look like a dummy in a clothing store window.

He got into his golden chariot with the diamond-set wheels and went round the track in a way to set the bleachers crazy. At breakneck speed he galloped over the rose-lined avenues of sensuous pleasures that opened for him in every direction, looking as if they led straight to paradise; but ere long his shining car of delight lost a wheel and he was down in the mud again, and crying out to any who might be following in his wake:

"Go back! Don't come this way, for here all is vanity and vexation of spirit!"

Then he took to wine and the rosiest kind of dissipation. He hit up the booze. He tried a lot of things. He had a great natatorium built, that was supported by great lions. Then he began to love many strange women, laying hold on folly with both hands. That's where he struck out. He had seven hundred wives and three hundred concubines, but soon had to give the same verdict as before, and again cry out:

"Vanity, vanity; all is vanity!"

Then he thinks he has discovered something really substantial, and so goes to building great works and houses, chief of which is the magnificent temple, still called by his name. It required seven years to build it, and took the combined efforts of one hundred and eighty-three thousand Jews and strangers to do the work. It took ten thousand men eleven years to cut the trees. There were eighty thousand hewers of wood, and seventy thousand burden bearers. There were eighty thousand squared stones, all so perfectly shaped in the quarries that the sound of neither hammer nor mallet was heard in putting them together in the temple.

At the completion of the work there was a feast of seven days at its dedication, and Solomon sacrificed one hundred and twenty thousand sheep and twenty thousand oxen.

The temple was built of white marble, so artfully joined that it appeared like one stone. The roof was of olive wood, covered with pure gold. That is where the idea

"WOMEN ONLY" MEETING, THOUSANDS BEING TURNED
AWAY.

of covering the domes of many of our capitol buildings with gold leaf originated. When the sunshine fell on the temple its splendor was so dazzling that the eyes were almost blinded.

The temple courts and apartments could house three hundred thousand people. There were fourteen hundred and fifty-three columns of Parian marble; twenty-nine hundred and six pilasters or columns. Over three billion dollars' worth of gold was used. One billion dollars' worth of silver was used on the floors and walls, which were overlaid with gold and silver.

There were two hundred targets of beaten gold, with six hundred shekels of gold in each target. There were three hundred targets with three hundred shekels in each target. There were three hundred shields of beaten gold, with three pounds of gold in each shield, and the value of the gold that came to Solomon in one year was about twenty millions of dollars. When the temple was dedicated the glory of God filled it.

Then Solomon turned his great talent and wealth toward making a beautiful Jerusalem, by planting vineyards and laying out gardens that were like Fairyland, and then like a tale of magic he produced orchards, in which he had a great collection of the finest and rarest trees in all the world. Trees from every clime, and flowers of every kind and hue were there, and all these were kept green and beautiful by irrigation from artificial lakes. It is doubtful if the world had ever seen greater beauty than Solomon with his unlimited power produced in Jerusalem at that time, but even all this pleased his fancy only for a little while, and soon he seems to have nothing but dust in his mouth, and again cries out:

"All is vanity!"

But almost immediately he seems to have taken up another whim, and says:

" I got me servants and maidens, and also had great possessions of great and small cattle, above all that were in Jerusalem before me. I gathered me also silver and gold, and the peculiar treasure of kings, and of the provinces. I got me men singers and women singers, and the delights of the sons of men, as musical instruments, and that of all sorts," meaning, no doubt, that he became an art collector, and began to feed on the beautiful, the artistic and esthetic, somewhat as millionaires are doing now, securing for himself the very best to be had in painting, old china, bric-à-brac, sculpture, musical instruments, singers and performers, and then at voluptuous ease he would lie on a princely couch that seemed almost to float in the air, and drink to the full all he could get out of them in the way of enjoyment.

But presently he is again almost dying with disappointment, and crying out in the same old doleful tone:

" All is vanity and vexation of spirit! "

Meaning that there was nothing in it all but an empty puff of air that could only fill a bubble for a moment. And then he goes on to say:

" So I was great, and increased more than all that were before me in Jerusalem; and whatever mine eyes desired I kept not from them. I withheld not my heart from joy; for my heart rejoiced in all my labor. Then I looked on all the works my hands had wrought, and on the labor that I had labored to do, and——

" Behold, all was vanity and vexation of spirit, and there was no profit under the sun! "

And so this wise and honored and wealthy man goes on drinking first from one golden cup and then another, only to dash them all away as soon as tasted in bitter disappointment, and then after he had tried them all, to say, "Not one can satisfy!" confirming what his father David had said in the statement, "The young lions do lack and suffer hunger," and just what every millionaire on earth to-day knows from his own experience.

To find starvation of the most awful kind to-day, don't go down into the slums, but go to the people who are enormously wealthy. Andrew Carnegie says there are no happy millionaires, and Andy ought to know, for he's got the dough. John D. Rockefeller has about as good as confessed that he got more out of the first thousand dollars he made than out of any ten millions he has made since, and to-day he is perhaps the hungriest man in all the world.

Every man wants to be satisfied. I do. So do you. Every one is reaching out for happiness and peace and rest. There are men before me who have tried many things in pursuit of happiness. You have climbed high and you have probed deep, and some of you have not found what you have sought. All who are here are on the verge of eternity. The past is simply a memory, the future an uncertainty. No matter how old you are; no matter if your hair is gray; no matter what your bank account may be; some of you must say, "I have not found happiness. I am a failure. My life has been a failure. All is vanity and vexation of spirit!"

Why don't you be a man? Why don't you show a man's courage, and take up the cross of the Son of God? Why don't you rise to what you might be? We were all meant for better things. You were never meant for the slop and the swill barrels of the devil. Why do you let the devil control you? Why do you let him make you a pawn on the board on which he plays his game?

Why do you spend your money for that which is

not bread? Is there any bread in rum? Ask the poor fellows who have been spending their earnings for drink during all these years. Ask their wives and their children. No bread for them. Ask the saloon-keeper. There is bread in it for him, but none for those who drink what he sells.

But to go back to Solomon's doleful cry of "All is vanity!" What does it mean? Was Solomon a dyspeptic, as most millionaires are? Have you ever noticed that it takes more religion to make a dyspeptic smile than it does to make a healthy man shout? Was there something wrong with Solomon's liver, or what was the matter? Was the trouble all with Solomon, or is all creation out of joint? Is there no good to be found in any of the things with which he employed his time? Is going to school no better than wasting time in idleness? Does a keen appreciation of the beautiful carry with it a curse and not a blessing? Is there no benefit in architecture, music or sculpture? Is there nothing but evil in wealth, wisdom and high station in life? Was Solomon really starving while apparently feeding on the finest of the wheat? He said so many things that appear to contradict all he said about vanity and vexation of spirit—and so what does it mean?

But wait a moment. Here is something that seems to throw light on the matter. When Solomon says, "All is vanity," he also says, "under the sun," and that shows the standpoint from which he drew his conclusions. What we see as we go through life always depends upon where we stand to look. Many a man who tries to talk as if he were standing on a mountain, shows by what he says that he is up to his eyes in the mud.

When a man tells you that the whisky business is a good thing for the country, you know that he is looking at things through the eyes of a brewer or a saloon-keeper, and not through the eyes of a father who has a son that has become a drunkard.

When a man tells you that he don't believe in foreign missions, you know that he don't know any more about what pure and undefiled religion is than a jack rabbit knows about running for president. From what he says you know the viewpoint from which he has come to his conclusion. To know a man's viewpoint is to know why he sees the thing he claims to see, and now we know why Solomon said:

" All is vanity and vexation of spirit! " It was because he was looking at things from the viewpoint of " under the sun." As if a man could tell what a rainbow were like while standing on his head in a dark cellar.

In the little book of Ecclesiastes, from which the text is taken, the expression " under the sun " occurs thirty-one times, as if Solomon wanted every one to understand that what he said therein was said from the standpoint of low ground. The great king was looking at things from a low, sensual, materialistic plane, and from that viewpoint every word he said was true. Take away God, take away the Bible, take away inspiration and revelation, take away all hope of a better life in the world to come —destroy all thought of resurrection, and put in its place nothing but hopeless and endless night, and you have nothing left that is worth living for. The life of the greatest and wisest man is then no better than that of a fool. The best fruits of the world would then turn to ashes on the lips, and it were better to die than to live.

Blot out everything except what we can know through our senses, and keep from us all light from a source higher than the sun, and the very best this life can give is worse than nothing at all. Destroy in every man the divine spark that tells him there is a God, and that there is a beyond, and every grave would hold a suicide. Let all hope die, and despair would reign.

We have only begun to know a little about the soul when we discover that nothing under the sun can satisfy it. It was this great truth Solomon began to realize after he found nothing but disappointment in the very best the world could give him. Under the sun nothing lasts; nothing endures; nothing satisfies. No sooner do we begin to think we have a thing safe forever than it is gone. We love but to lose. Whatever we have is ours but for one brief moment, and the anguish of our loss is a wound that never heals. No happiness is possible without the hope of certainty, and the thing we feel we must have mocks us as it flies. No fountain under the sun can hold enough to satisfy an immortal spirit, and that very fact proves us to be spirits in prison while we are here.

All the gold mines in the world have not given up treasure enough to satisfy the man who has a greed for gain. The man with a hunger for honor and distinction has never been able to get enough of it, and the same can be said of everything else for which men strive and struggle and destroy each other and themselves.

Nothing this world can give is worth while, unless while living in it we can have more than is revealed by the light of the sun. Destroy the Bible and all faith in God, and we might as well eat, drink and be merry and die. Nothing will do unless it can give us the wings of the morning and let us mount higher than the sun, for what can a mole know about the sunrise, or a man in a pit know about the beauty of the mountains? No heaven we can build for ourselves without God can be more than a little ante-room to hell. Without God and revelation and the Bible and hope of heaven, all is indeed vanity and vexation of spirit.

But at last Solomon spreads the wings of faith and gets higher than the sun, and when he does the change in his viewpoint changes the meaning of life, for now he can see with a clear eye.

I know a man who through some difficulty with his vision can see scarcely anything a little distance away, but one day he went up in a balloon, and when over a half-mile high he could see like a bird. In fact he could see better than he had ever believed anybody could see, and it was that way with Solomon when he reached the place where his faith could lay hold on God.

Listen to this, and note how his vision has expanded, and his sight cleared up: " Surely I know (no uncertainty about that) that it shall be well with them that fear God." There is no more talk about everything being vanity now, and the reason is because at last he has a viewpoint higher than the sun, as is always the case with even the humblest man who has faith in God. Solomon can now see that nothing good is ever lost, and that bread cast on the waters is sure to return after many days. He now sees that wisdom is better than weapons of war, the plain meaning of which in our day is that good common-sense is better protection than a slungshot. And then, to sum up, he closes the book by saying:

" Let us hear the conclusion of the whole matter: Fear God, and keep His commandments, for this is the whole duty of man. For God shall bring every work into judgment, with every secret thing, whether it be good, or whether it be evil." And there is no vanity about anything God does.

And now let us employ our time for a little while

with some of the men who have looked at life from a viewpoint higher than the sun. It was this that kept Noah working away on the ark for a hundred and twenty years, without seeing a flash of lightning or hearing a clap of thunder. Had he been living only for what he could see, it would never have been said of him that " he was a just man and perfect, and walked with God." The man who walks with God will not spend much time in thinking about the bugs that may be creeping under his feet.

Abraham was another man who had a faith that lifted him higher than the sun, when looking for " a city which had foundations, whose maker and builder was God." You never hear a word from that grand old man about all being vanity and vexation of spirit.

And then there was Moses. He had a vision that pierced the clouds and went far beyond the sun, when he saw that " the reproach of Christ " would bring him greater and more lasting riches than the treasures of Egypt, that he might have had by simply folding his arms and doing nothing. But he endured as seeing Him who is invisible, and that made it easy for him to refuse to be called the son of Pharaoh's daughter. Neither was he looking from the low plane of " under the sun," when in bidding farewell to the army he had brought out of Egypt, he said: " The eternal God is thy refuge, and underneath are the everlasting arms." A man must have a sweep of faith reaching higher than the sun before he can say things like that.

There is not a word about " under the sun " in the chapter where grand old General Joshua says, " As for me and my house, we will serve the Lord," and no such words as " vanity and vexation of spirit " ever fell from the lips of that great captain of iron courage.

MR. AND MRS. SUNDAY LEADING 22,000 PEOPLE IN SUNDAY SCHOOL PARADE, AT WILKES-BARRE, PA.

Samuel was looking at things from much higher than the sun when he said, "To obey is better than sacrifice," and so was Job when he said, "I will trust Him though He slay me," and "I know that my redeemer lives!"

Ezra was not standing on low ground when "he prepared his heart to seek the law of the Lord, and to do it," or when he said, "The hand of our God is upon all of them for good that seek Him, and His power and His wrath is against all them that forsake Him." The same was true of Nehemiah, when, in building up the wall that was broken down, he said, "I am doing a great work." From "under the sun" it would have looked very small.

David was looking from higher than the sun, or he could never have said, "The angel of the Lord encampeth round about them that fear Him, and delivereth them. O taste, and see that the Lord is good; blessed is the man that trusteth in Him!" And Daniel had a vision that swept far higher than the sun when he went to the lions' den with no more anxiety than you and I would go to dinner.

Stephen's viewpoint was from much higher than anywhere "under the sun," when he cried out, "Behold, I see the heavens opened, and the Son of man standing on the right hand of God!" and then went to his cruel death with the light of heaven on his face.

And Paul was looking from higher than the stars, or he could never have said: "For we know that if our earthly house of this tabernacle were dissolved, we have a building of God, an house not made with hands, eternal in the heavens!"

And so it was also with John the beloved, when near the close of his long and busy life he took up the much worn pen with which he had written so much that will still be bright when the stars are dim, and wrote the precious words that have been shining down the centuries ever since: "Behold what manner of love the Father hath bestowed upon us, that we should be called the sons of God; therefore the world knoweth us not, because it knew Him not. Beloved, now are we the sons of God, and it doth not yet appear what we shall be; but we know that when He shall appear, we shall be like Him; for we shall see Him as He is!"

And then still later, when a white-haired prisoner on the Isle of Patmos, and just before he left the world to be forever with the Lord, John again had a vision of things infinitely higher than the sun, and once more took up the stylus and wrote: "And I saw heaven opened, and behold a white horse; and He that sat upon him was called Faithful and True, and in righteousness He doth judge and make war. . . . And He was clothed with a vesture dipped in blood; and His name is called the Word of God. . . . And He hath on His vesture and on His thigh a name written, King of Kings and Lord of Lords!"

Jude also was looking from very much higher than the sun when he declared with unhesitating confidence: "That He is able to keep you from falling, and to present you faultless before the presence of His glory with exceeding joy."

And O how much higher than the sun was Jesus looking from when He said: "Let not your heart be troubled; ye believe in God, believe also in Me. In My Father's house are many mansions: if it were not so, I would have told you. I go to prepare a place for you, and if I go and prepare a place for you, I will come again, and receive you unto Myself; that where I am, there ye may be also."

And then, when after the shame of the cross and the grave, He stood on resurrection ground, how infinitely far above the sun was His eye fixed when He said to the eleven faithful ones: "All power is given unto Me in heaven and in earth; go ye therefore, and teach all nations, baptising them in the name of the Father, and of the Son, and of the Holy Ghost: teaching them to observe all things whatsoever I have commanded you; and lo, I am with you always, even unto the end of the world."

And thank God the time will surely come, when in our vision we shall not be confined to the low plane described as "under the sun," but when with Him in whom we have believed we shall be lifted "far above all principality and power, and might and dominion," and be with Him forever in heavenly places, where we shall no more see as through a glass darkly, but face to face, and where we shall know as we are known.

WONDERFUL

His name shall be called Wonderful.—Isa. 9:6.

IN olden times all names meant something, and this is still the case among Indians and all other people who are living in a primitive way. Whenever you know an Indian's name and the meaning of it, you know something about the Indian. Such names as Kill Deer, Eagle Eye, Buffalo Face and Sitting Bull tell us something about the men who possessed them.

This tendency to use names that are expressive still crops out in camp life, and whenever men are thrown together in an unconventional way. In mining, military and lumber camps nearly every man has a nickname that indicates some peculiarity or trait of character. Usually a man's nickname is nearer the real man than his right name.

All of our family names to-day had their origin in something that meant something. All Bible names have a meaning, and when you read the Scriptures it will always help you to a better understanding of their meaning to look up the definition of all proper names.

There are two hundred and fifty-six names given in the Bible for the Lord Jesus Christ, and I suppose this was because He was infinitely beyond all that any one name could express.

Of the many names given to Christ it is my purpose at this time to briefly consider this one: " His name shall be called Wonderful." Let us look into it somewhat and see whether He was true to the name given Him in a prophecy eight hundred years before He was born. Does the name fit Him? Is it such a name as He ought to have?

Wonderful means something that is transcendently beyond the common; something that is away beyond the ordinary. It means something that is altogether unlike anything else. We say that Yellowstone Park, Niagara Falls and the Grand Cañon of the Colorado are wonderful because there is nothing else like them.

When David killed Goliath with his sling he did a wonderful thing, because nobody else ever did anything like it. It was wonderful that the Red Sea should open to make a highway for Israel, and wonderful that the sun should stand still for Joshua. Let us see whether Jesus was true to His name.

His birth was wonderful, for no other ever occurred that was like it. It was wonderful in that He had but one human parent, and so inherited the nature of man and the nature of God. He came to be the Prince of princes, and the King of kings, and yet His birth was not looked forward to in glad expectation, as the birth of a prince usually is in the royal palace, and celebrated with marked expressions of joy all over the country, as has repeatedly happened within the recollection of many who are here.

There was no room for Him at the inn, and He had to be born in a stable, and cradled in a manger, and yet angels proclaimed His birth with joy from the sky, to a few humble shepherds in sheepskin coats, who were watching their flocks by night.

Mark how He might have come with all the pomp and glory of the upper world. It would have been a great condescension for Him to have been born in a palace, rocked in a golden cradle and fed with golden spoons, and to have had the angels come down and be His nurses. But He gave up all the glory of that world, and was born of a poor woman, and His cradle was a manger.

Think what He had come for. He had come to bless, and not to curse; to lift up, and not to cast down. He had come to seek and to save that which was lost. To give sight to the blind; to open prison doors and set captives free; to reveal the Father's love; to give rest to the weary; to be a blessing to the whole world, and yet there was no room for Him. He came to do that, and yet many of you have no room for Him in your hearts.

His birth was also wonderful in this, that the wise men of the East were guided from far across the desert to His birthplace by a star. Nothing like this ever announced the coming of any one else into this world. As soon as His birth was known the king of the country sought His life, and ordered the slaughter of the Innocents at Bethlehem. The babies were the first Christian martyrs.

His character was wonderful, for no other has ever approached it in perfection. It is wonderful that the greatest character ever known should have come out of such obscurity, to become the most famous in all history. That such a time and such a country and such a people should have produced Jesus Christ can be accounted for on no other ground than His divinity. On his return from a trip to the Holy Land a minister was asked what had made the greatest impression upon him while there. " Nazareth," he answered, and for this reason:

" The same kind of people are living there to-day as in the time of Jesus, and they are about the worst specimens of humanity I have seen anywhere. Lazy, lustful, ignorant and unspeakably wicked, and to think of His coming out from such a people is to me a sure proof of His divinity. Had I not been a believer in His divinity before going there, I should have to believe in it now."

His life was wonderful. Wonderful for its unselfishness, its sinlessness and its usefulness. Even His enemies could not bring against Him any graver charge than that He claimed God for His Father, and that He would do good on the Sabbath day. Not the slightest evidence of selfishness or self-interest can be found in the story of His life. He was always helping others, but not once did He do anything to help Himself. He had the power to turn stones into bread, but went hungry forty days without doing it. While escaping from enemies who were determined to put Him to death He saw a man who had been blind from birth, and stopped to give him sight, doing so at the risk of His life. He never sought His own in any way, but lived for others every day of His life. His first miracle was performed, not before a multitude to spread His own fame, but in a far-away hamlet, to save a peasant's wife from humiliation. He had compassion on the hungry multitude and wept over Jerusalem, but He never had any mercy on Himself.

His teaching was wonderful. It was wonderful for the way in which He taught; for its simplicity and clearness, and adaptation to the individual. Nowhere do you find Him seeking the multitude, but He never avoided the individual. And His teaching was always adapted to the comprehension of those whom He taught. It is said that the common people heard Him gladly, and this shows that they understood what He said. He put the cookies on the lower shelf. No man had to take a dictionary with him when he went to hear the Sermon on the Mount. He illustrated His thought and made plain

His meaning by the most wonderful word-pictures. The preacher who would reach the people must have something to say, and know how to say it so that those who hear will know just what he means.

Jesus made His meaning clear by using plenty of illustrations. He didn't care a rap what the scribes and Pharisees thought about it, or said about it. He wanted the people to know what He meant, and that is why He was always so interesting. The preacher who can't make his preaching interesting has no business in the pulpit. If he can't talk over ten minutes without making people begin to snap their watches and go to yawning all over the house, he has misunderstood the Lord about his call to preach. Jesus was interesting because He could put the truth before people in an interesting way. We are told that without a parable He spake not to any man. He made people see things, and see them clearly. It is wonderful that this humble Galilean peasant, who may never have gone to school a day in His life, should have made Himself a Teacher of teachers for all time. The pedagogy of to-day is modeling after the manner of Christ closer and closer every day.

He was wonderful in His originality. The originality of Jesus is a proof of His divinity. The human mind cannot create anything in an absolute sense. It can build out of almost any kind of material, but it cannot create. There is no such thing as out-and-out originality belonging to man. You cannot imagine anything that does not resemble something you have previously seen or heard of.

I grant that you can take a cow and a horse and a dog and a sheep and from them make animals enough to fill Noah's ark, but you must have the cow and the horse and the dog and the sheep for a beginning. Everything you make will simply be a modification of the various forms and properties of them.

There is said to be nothing new under the sun, and there is a sense in which it is true. Everything is the outgrowth of something else. The first railway cars looked like the old stage-coaches, and the first automobiles looked like carriages. It is that way about everything. No man ever made a book, or even a story, that was altogether unlike all others.

The stories we hear to-day on the Irish and Dutch are older than the Irish and Dutch. You can find stories like them in the earliest literature, but you can't find any stories anywhere in any literature that even in the remotest way resemble the parables of Jesus. Such parables as the prodigal son and the Good Samaritan are absolutely new creations, and so proclaim Jesus as divine, because He could create.

His teaching was wonderful, not only in the way He taught, but in what He taught. He taught that He was greater than Moses. Think of the audacity of it! Making such claims as that to the Jews, who regarded Moses as being almost divine. Think of the audacity of some man of obscure and humble parentage standing before us Americans and trying to make us think he was greater than George Washington.

Jesus also declared that He fulfilled the prophecies and the law of Moses, and the only effort He ever made to prove His claim was to point to the works that He did. The first thing an impostor always does is to overprove his case. Jesus never turned His hand over to try to convince His enemies that He was the Christ. You have to explain a coal-oil lamp, but you don't need to waste any breath in giving information about the power of the sun. The springtime will do that by making all nature burst into bud, flower and leaf, and the power of Christ is shown just as convincingly in the changed lives of men and women who believe in Him.

Jesus taught that all would be lost who did not believe on Him. I have seen multitudes of saved people, but I have yet to see one who did not get his salvation by believing on Christ. Find the place in this world that comes the nearest to being like hell itself, and you will find it filled with those who are haters of Jesus Christ. You can't argue it. Go into saloons, gambling hells, and such places, and the people you find there are all haters of Jesus Christ, and the more of them you find the more the place in which you find them will be like hell itself.

Jesus taught that He was equal to God. He said, "He that hateth Me hateth My Father also" (John 15:23). Did you ever know of anybody else making such claims? He said, "Come unto Me, all ye that labor and are heavy laden, and I will give you rest." Offering to bear the burden of the whole world. Think of it! He said, "I am come that they might have life, and that they might have it more abundantly." And He said, "I am the resurrection and the life; and he that believeth in Me, though he were dead, yet shall he live. And whosoever liveth and believeth in Me shall never die." Surely He was wonderful in what He taught.

It is not surprising that He so stirred them in the Capernaum synagogue, where He taught them not as the scribes, but as one having authority. Is it any wonder that they were right after Him for heresy? Let any one to-day begin to teach in our churches something as entirely new as the teachings of Jesus were, and see what will happen.

He was wonderful in what He prophesied of Himself. He foretold how He would die, and when He would die.

BIDDING THE SUNDAYS GOOD-BY AT CLOSE OF A CAMPAIGN.

It was wonderful that He should have been betrayed into the hands of those who sought His life, by one of His own trusted disciples, and wonderful that He should have been sold for so low a price.

Wonderful, too, that He should have been condemned to death in the way in which He was, by both the religious and civil authorities, and on the testimony of false witnesses, in the name of God, when all the laws of God were defied in the trial. It was wonderful that He was tormented and tortured so cruelly before being sent to the cross, and that He should have been put to death in the brutal manner in which He was. The time of His death was also wonderful; on the day of the Passover, thus Himself becoming the real Passover, to which the passover lamb had so long pointed.

The great publicity of His death was also wonderful. It is doubtful if any other death was ever witnessed by so many people. Hundreds of thousands of people were in Jerusalem, who had come from everywhere to attend the Passover. The sky was darkened, and the sun hid his face from the awful scene. A great earthquake shook the city; the dead came out of their graves, and went into the city, appearing unto many, and the veil of the temple was rent from top to bottom. And remember that up to that time no eye had been allowed to look behind that veil, except that of the high priest, and then only once a year, on the great Day of Atonement.

His resurrection was wonderful. He had foretold it to His disciples, and had done so frequently, always saying, whenever He spoke of His death, that He would rise again on the third day, and yet every one of them appeared to forget all about it, and not one of them was expecting it. None of them thought of going to the sepulcher on the morning of the third day, except the women, and they only to prepare His body more fully for the grave.   Womanhood has always been on the firing line.

This shows how fully they had abandoned all hope when they saw Him dead.   Some left the city, for we are told of two who went to Emmaus.   The manner of His resurrection was godlike.   No human mind could ever have imagined such a scene.   Had some man described it in the way in which he thought it should have occurred, he would have had earthquakes and thunders and a great commotion in the heavens.   A sound like that of the last trump would have proclaimed to all the terrified inhabitants of Jerusalem that He was risen.   But see how far different it was.

An angel rolled away the stone from the mouth of the sepulcher as quietly as the opening of the buds in May, and the women, who were early there, found no disorder in the grave, but the linen clothes with which they had tenderly robed His body were neatly folded and tidily placed.

And then how wonderful are the recorded appearances after the resurrection, again so different from what man would have had them.   He appeared to every one of His friends, and to His best friends, but not a single one of His enemies got to see Him.   I know that this story of the resurrection is true, because none but God would have had things happen in the order that they did, and in the way in which they occurred.   Had the story been false the record would have made Jesus go to Pilate and the high priest, and to the others who had put Him to death, to prove that He was risen.

The effect of His teaching upon the world has been wonderful.   Remember that He left no great colleges to promulgate His doctrines, but committed them to a few humble fishermen, whose names are now the most illustrious in all history. Looked at from the human side alone, how great was the probability that everything He had said would be forgotten within a few years. He never wrote a sermon. He published no books. Not a thing He said was engraved upon stone or scrolled upon brass, and yet His doctrines have endured for two thousand years. They have gone to the ends of the earth, and have wrought miracles wherever they have gone. They have lifted nations out of darkness and degradation and sin, and have made the wilderness to blossom as the rose.

When Jesus began His ministry Rome ruled the world, and her invincible legions were everywhere, but now through the teachings of the humble Galilean peasant, whom her minions put to death, her power and her religion are gone. The great temple of Diana of the Ephesians is in ruins, and no worshipper of her can be found.

When Jesus fed the five thousand with a few loaves and fishes, and healed the poor woman who touched the hem of His garment, there wasn't a church, or a hospital, or an insane asylum, or other eleemosynary institution in the world, and now they are nearly as countless as the sands upon the seashore. When the bright cloud hid Him from the gaze of those who loved Him with a devotion that took them to martyrdom, the only record of His sayings was graven upon their hearts, but now libraries are devoted to the consideration of them. No words were ever so weighty or so weighed as those of Him who was so poor that He had not where to lay His head. The scholarship of the world has sat at His feet with bared head, and has been compelled to say again and again, " Never man spake as He spake." His utterances have been translated into every known tongue, and have carried healing on their wings wherever they have gone. No other book has ever had a tithe of the circulation of that which contains His words, and not only that, but His thoughts and the story of His life are so interwoven in all literature that if a man should never read a line in the Bible, and yet be a reader at all he could not remain ignorant of the Christ.

He is true to His name because He is a wonderful Savior now. You have only to lift your eyes and look about you to see that His wonderful salvation is going on everywhere to-day. This vast audience throws the lie back into your teeth when you say the religion of Jesus Christ is dying out. There has never been a time when the love of Christ gripped the hearts of humanity as it does to-day.

When John the Baptist, in prison, sent two of his disciples to Jesus, saying: " Art thou He that should come, or do we look for another?" Jesus sent this answer to John: " The blind receive their sight; the lame walk, the lepers are cleansed, and the deaf hear; the dead are raised up, and the poor have the gospel preached unto them "; and that test of His power is as apparent in nearly every part of the world to-day as it was in Galilee. If you have eyes to see the works of God, you will always find them going on. The heavens declare the glory of God, but there are people so blind they can't see anything but a spell of weather in the rainbow.

Jerry McAuley in prison, a man who had lived by crime, and who had never heard the name of God outside of profanity; as blind and dead to anything good as a stone, one Sunday in the prison chapel heard a verse of Scripture quoted that took hold of his attention. He thought he would like to see it and read it for himself.

So he took the Bible in his cell and began to search for it. He didn't know but one sure way to find it, and that was to begin at the first verse in the Bible and read straight on until he came to it. The verse he wanted was in Hebrews, away over in the back part of the New Testament.

Jerry read on, chapter after chapter, and day after day, looking for that verse, but long before he found it he found Jesus Christ—just as some of you would do if you would only be honest with God, and give Him a chance at you by reading His word. From that time on everybody who came near Jerry McAuley knew that the eyes of the man born blind had been opened in him. He started the Water Street Mission in New York, where I don't believe a service was ever held in which somebody was not converted.

Any number of men who were headed straight for the devil are preaching the gospel to-day because they were stopped by the light of God and the voice of His Christ as suddenly at St. Paul was. Yes, He is a wonderful Savior because He is able to save to the uttermost now.

A man would be a great surgeon who could save ninety per cent. of those upon whom he operated, but mark this: Jesus Christ never lost a case. He never found a case that was too hard for Him. His disciples were continually finding cases they thought were hopeless, and this shows how little they knew Him while He was with them.

Jesus never sent anybody away who came honestly and earnestly seeking His help. They brought to Him all kinds of desperate cases, but at a word or a touch from Him their troubles were all gone. The hardest cases were no more difficult for Him than the easiest, and the same is true to-day, for there is no change in Him. He is the same yesterday, to-day and forever. He can save the scarlet sinner—the man who commits murder —as easily as He can the woman who cheats at cards.

He is a wonderful Savior, too, because He can save so quickly. Quicker than thought He can give you life. It is only, look and live. As quick as you can come He receives you, and as quickly as you could receive a present you had been wanting for years, you can have salvation. " Him that cometh to Me I will in nowise cast out." " To as many as received Him, to them gave He power to become the sons of God." No need of taking very much time about that.

In a meeting Thomas Harrison was holding, a railroad engineer came forward with his watch in his hand and said, " Mr. Harrison, can I be saved in ten minutes? I must leave here to take my train out then."

" Yes," replied Harrison, " you can be saved in ten seconds." The man dropped on his knees, was quickly saved and had seven minutes to spare. A conductor on a fast Pennsylvania train, in Ohio, was converted while crossing a bridge fifty feet long, when going at the rate of a mile a minute. Yes, indeed, He is a wonderful Savior because He can save so quickly.

Moody used to tell of a banker in San Francisco, who was awakened in the night by a burglar at his bedside. The robber held a revolver almost against his face, and said, " If you move I'll kill you!" The banker said, " God have mercy on my soul!" and knocked the burglar down before he could pull the trigger, and was soundly converted before the man struck the floor, as his life afterward proved.

And now I come to the last evidence I will give you that He is true to His name, and that is—

He is a wonderful Savior because He saved me. There is nothing that can be so convincing to a man as his own experience. I do not know that I am the son of my mother any more certainly than I know that I am a child of God, and I do not know that I have been born in a natural way any more convincingly than I know that I have been born of the Spirit.

And now let me ask you this: Has this wonderful Savior saved you? Do you know Him as your Savior? Have you ever given Him your case? When the proof is so overwhelming that He does save, and has been saving for centuries, and that none have ever been saved or ever can be saved except through Him, is it not wonderful that any one can be indifferent to the claims of Jesus Christ?

THE BILLY SUNDAY CLUBS

Out of the furnace of revival fires have come the metals which have been welded into the Billy Sunday Clubs. They are composed of men who have been converted or quickened in spirit by these meetings. This organization has developed spontaneously out of an inherent need for unity of action among kindred souls. They are each independent, being free to elect their own officers, committees and in all respects determine their own course of action. But it is significant that each one actually does very similar things; the object being to advance the Kingdom of Heaven in the hearts of their fellows. They are essentially soul winners never omitting, whenever opportunity presents to give their individual testimony on the side of Christ.

To the convert all things are new. The change in his outlook is a violent one. The more sinful a man has been the greater the shock. It is like one long imprisoned being set free; or like one blind, restored to sight. Bringing blind souls out of spiritual darkness is God's greatest miracle. Now these converts are in very great need of special care at first. They are learning to walk in new paths and no doubt will be inclined to stumble as obstacles present themselves. He, with great enthusiasm, has an urge to do things for the kingdom and has great difficulty in gearing himself up to existing organizations. Should the formality or the red tape get the best of him he is in danger. With the Billy Sunday Clubs to fall back on he is more likely to be carried over this crucial period and become an active dependable Christian worker. In union is strength. The convert needs a lot of strength; all that he had, all that God gives, all that his fellow men can offer.

We should not be surprised, then that clubs so composed have accomplished great religious work because the spirit of the Master working in remade men is performing miracles in the hearts of tens of thousands.

So the Billy Sunday clubs are spreading and their work is growing day by day. They form a fraternity, but their God-given ritual is anything but secret. Indeed they have the great desire "to tell the world." They are a portion of God's advertising staff and are working under divine approval. It is an honor and education and a great inspiration to belong to a Billy Sunday Club. Activity is their mainspring and dominant characteristic. Their motto could be, "Keeping Busy For God."

Religion is peculiar in that in order to keep it we are under the necessity of constantly giving it away. The more we give the more we get. It is a kind of a personal self-realization for which no material wealth or social fame has any substitute.

The Billy Sunday Clubs should be encouraged everywhere for they are doing a work that is needed in each community and each member is himself wonderfully blessed.

For the past 2 or 3 years these clubs have been sending representatives to Winona to meet in a fraternal spirit and gain inspiration from the Bible conference there. This has been very interesting.

Billy Sunday Clubs have been organized in, Atlanta,

Ga., Bluefield, Va., Roanoke, Va., Spartansburg, S. C., Syracuse, N. Y., Dayton, Ohio, Boston, Mass., Cincinnati, Ohio, Logan, W. Va., Buffalo N. Y., Kansas City, Mo., Beckley, W. Va., Sioux City, Ia., Columbia, South Carolina, Omaha, Nebraska, Trenton, N. J., Wilkes-Barre, Pa., Scranton, Pa., Richmond, Ind., Knoxville Tenn., Bristol, Tenn., Wichita, Kans., Morristown, Tenn., New York City, N. Y., Tulsa, Okla., Oklahoma City, Okla., Jacksonville, Florida.

PRINTED IN THE UNITED STATES OF AMERICA